MODELING THE OIL INDUSTRY

Jeff Wilson

Acknowledgements:

Several individuals helped me with this book by finding and providing photographs and prototype information. I thank Ted Culotta of Speedwitch Media (speedwitchmedia.com), Cody Grivno, Scott A. Hartley, the late J. David Ingles, Keith Kohlmann, Mont Switzer, and Jeff Teasley of Historic Aerials (historicaerials.com) for this. Many of the photos came from the David P. Morgan Library at Kalmbach Media; I'm always indebted to the photographers whose work resides there. I'm also thankful to the many photographers and companies that documented the industry (the refineries themselves as well as railcars), especially in the steam and early diesel eras.

Jeff Wilson

On the cover: Steam rises from tank cars on the cleaning track at the Humble refinery in Baytown, Texas, in December 1944. The tall structure in the background is a catalytic cracker, which separates crude oil into several different usable components. *Standard Oil Co.*

Back cover, top: Workers prepare to unload oil from a set of General American TankTrain cars, which are connected with hoses, at Essexville, Mich., in 1978. *George Drury*

Back cover, bottom: A Norfolk Southern train hauling crude oil from North Dakota's Bakken oil fields prepares for unloading at a refinery in Delaware City, Del., in 2013. *Michael S. Murray*

At right: A worker turns the air/vent line valve under the bonnet of a liquefied petroleum gas (LPG) pressure car. The two valves to the side govern the product lines; the safety valve is behind the air line. See Chapter 6. *Russell Lee, Library of Congress*

Kalmbach Media
21027 Crossroads Circle
Waukesha, Wisconsin 53186
www.KalmbachHobbyStore.com

Published in 2024
28 27 26 25 24 1 2 3 4 5

Manufactured in China

ISBN: 978-162700-975-1
EISBN: 978-162700-976-8

Editor: Steven Otte
Book Design: Lisa Bergman

Library of Congress Control Number: 2023941816

Contents

Modeling the oil industry

The petroleum industry has been tied to railroading since the first successful oil well was drilled in Pennsylvania in 1859. Since then, railroads have carried crude oil and finished products such as gasoline, lube oil, and liquified petroleum gas among oilfields, refineries, local fuel dealers, large pipeline terminals, and innumerable final customers and industrial users.

The industry offers myriad opportunities for modeling, regardless of the era, region, or specific railroad you model. Fuel dealers are located in towns of all sizes, and most of these were rail-served through the 1960s. Large refineries are located throughout the country, as are tank terminals that distribute products received via pipeline. Although these are large facilities, they can provide inspiration for modeling.

Refineries continue to ship products by rail, and many tank terminals do so, as well. This rail traffic, and the tank cars involved, can logically be incorporated onto almost any layout set anywhere in the country.

The cars that carry petroleum products are varied and make great modeling projects. From the steam era into the 1950s, most refined products traveled by general-purpose 50-ton tank cars, typically from 8,000 to 10,000 gallons in capacity. Although "plain" in many ways, many carried the logos or names of the oil companies that owned or leased them.

The tank cars carrying liquified gases (propane, butane, and blends known as "liquified petroleum gas," or LPG cars) were distinctive as well.

Tank cars have been spotted at a loading platform at a Baton Rouge, La., refinery, as a storage tank and catalytic cracking units loom in the distance. The image is from 1943, when railroads were hauling tremendous amounts of petroleum traffic during World War II. *Standard Oil Co.*

A tank car is being unloaded at right at a Pure jobber (local fuel dealer) in Racine, Wis., in 1955. Most local dealers were served by rail into the 1960s. *Bob Johnson, Keith Kohlmann collection*

As with other freight cars, tank cars grew in size starting in the 1960s. Although the expanding pipeline network has taken away most refined-product traffic, the emergence of new oil fields in the 2000s led to unit-train traffic in crude oil, carried by modern 20,000-gallon-plus tank cars. Railroads still carry plenty of LPG traffic in 33,000-gallon, high-pressure tank cars, as well as some gasoline traffic in general-purpose cars.

Part of what makes the oil industry so attractive to model are the dozens of companies with their colorful logos that have existed since the early 1900s. This was especially true from the 1920s through the 1960s, a period that I call the "classic era" of railroads and petroleum traffic.

Not that the modern era doesn't have its attractive modeling qualities, but the varied companies and the many small rail-served dealers make the classic era the period upon which this book focuses.

The 1950s and later saw the emergence of the petrochemical industry, with petroleum products used as feedstocks to produce a tremendous variety of chemicals and synthetic products. That industry is an entity unto itself, so we've kept the focus on the traditional business of crude oil, refineries, and refined products (gasoline, oil, LPG, kerosene).

The following chapters outline the history of the petroleum industry, examine the refining process, show how that process has evolved, and illustrate how refineries, local dealers, and pipeline terminals all worked with railroads to distribute products. Together these will offer many ideas you can incorporate into your model railroad and its operations.

A long string of tank cars awaits loading with crude oil at Spindletop, Texas, in 1901. The huge oil strike near Beaumont, Texas, led to the Gulf Coast region becoming a center of refining operations for the next century.
Library of Congress

CHAPTER ONE

History and oil field operations

The discovery of oil in Pennsylvania in 1859 was a momentous occasion, although few realized it at the time, calling Edwin Drake's well "Drake's Folly." Indeed, it took time to figure out what to do with all of the crude oil, and no one was sure whether the supply would last. Over the following decades the American oil industry boomed, thanks to growing population and the emergence of the gasoline-powered automobile. Oil companies became key customers for railroads, with tens of thousands of tank cars carrying millions of gallons of crude oil and finished products.

A unit train of crude oil in new Trinity-built tank cars rolls through New Castle, Del., on Norfolk Southern in 2013.
Michael S. Murray

Although long-distance pipelines and trucks began taking much of this business away from railroads by the 1950s, railroads still carry a significant amount of petroleum traffic. New oil fields and improved extraction technologies have led to an increase in crude oil traffic by rail, and railroads still haul some gasoline and other products as well as significant carloads of liquified petroleum gas (LPG).

The history of the oil industry could take up many volumes, and there are indeed hundreds of books and online sources that do that. So our summary will, of necessity, hit just the highlights. In this chapter we'll start with a brief look at the history of the petroleum industry, see how companies get oil from the ground, and examine how railroads became part of the process.

Early history

People were aware of oil and gas buried in the ground long before Drake began drilling. Some cultures have been using oil for thousands of years, but on a small, local level. Capturing oil, then processing and delivering it on a large scale, was something different.

The first refinery appeared in Pittsburgh in 1853, six years before Drake's well. The refinery was built by Samuel Kier, who was looking for a use for the oil that had been fouling his salt wells. Kier's experiments produced light oil from the crude, which he marketed for use in lamps. Colonel A.C. Ferris, who improved upon Kier's methods, is credited with the 1857 discovery that kerosene could be distilled from crude oil.

This kerosene found a ready market for use in lamps and lanterns, as it produced better light with less smoke than coal oil. Both were looked at as alternatives for whale oil, which at the time was regarded as the best fuel for lamps and lanterns. However, as population grew and demands for whale oil increased, it was becoming harder to get and more expensive.

Edwin Drake's company in 1859 began drilling a well near Titusville, Pa., an area where oil sometimes oozed out of the ground on its own (to the annoyance of farmers and local residents). Drake took advantage of a then-new technique of using a stationary steam engine to drive a pipe into the ground to tap the oil, as opposed to digging a pit or shaft. The going was slow—about three feet per day—but Drake struck an oil deposit at 69 feet. The oil began coming out of the pipe, eventually at the rate of about 20 barrels per day (the 42-gallon barrel remains the industry standard for measurement; the abbreviation for barrel is "bbl").

Drake's success would lead to other wells in the region, providing a ready supply of oil for refiners. The challenge then became how to process it efficiently. The first (and only) goal of early crude production was getting the kerosene out, which was not an easy task.

The first successful oil well in the U.S. was drilled by Edwin Drake in 1859 at Titusville, Pa. The well is shown here in 1861; Drake is at left with Peter Wilson.
John A. Mather, Library of Congress

Early petroleum refining techniques were primitive, slow, dirty, and dangerous. The first refineries consisted simply of a basic still: an open iron kettle of crude oil heated over an open flame. The lightest gas fractions evaporated, then gasoline rose to the top, which had to be skimmed off. Gasoline had no practical use at the time—it was volatile and explosive, and indeed it was responsible for disastrous results at some operations—and was burned off as waste. After the gasoline came the next-heaviest fraction, kerosene. It was again skimmed off and captured. Following that, the rest of the kettle was generally discarded and the process repeated with a fresh kettle of crude oil.

Within a few years, refiners found new products, capturing the lightest liquid fractions (napthas) for use as solvents, and processing the heavier fractions to make lubricating oils.

Railroads' initial role in the industry was getting crude oil from wells to refineries. These were generally short hauls, often no more than a few miles (Titusville to Pittsburgh was about 70 miles), but it was more efficient to do by railcar than by tanks on horse-drawn wagons. Shipping oil in barrels atop flatcars and gondolas was the first method, followed by pairs of vertical wood tanks built atop flatcars. Cars with iron and then steel horizontal tanks replaced earlier wood cars starting in the 1870s.

As the oil business grew, more wells were drilled, additional regions and oil fields were discovered, and refineries sprang up around the area. By 1866, just seven years after Drake drilled his first well, the Pittsburgh area alone had 60 refineries. Oil production in the U.S. went from 2,000 barrels in 1859 to 4.2 million barrels in 1869 and 19.9 million barrels in 1879.

The boom in the business spurred hundreds of small companies to dig wells, build refineries, and sell the products. The possibilities attracted large financial backers, and in 1863 John D. Rockefeller began dabbling in the industry, officially incorporating Standard Oil of Pennsylvania in 1870. Rockefeller quickly built his company into an empire by buying out or forcing out many smaller companies and expanding his own refining operations and marketing the resulting products. By 1890 Standard Oil controlled almost 90 percent of the

The Standard Oil of Indiana refinery at Wood River, Ill., near St. Louis was state-of-the-art when built in 1907. The horizontal stills at right, each marked by a smokestack for its furnace, were standard before fractionating towers were introduced.
Library of Congress

The first railroad tank cars were flatcars with pairs of vertical wooden tanks on the decks. Each tank holds about 40 barrels of oil. The photo dates to 1867. *Association of American Railroads*

U.S. oil business, most of which was, at the time, located in Pennsylvania and neighboring states. (See "Standard Oil monopoly and breakup" on page 15 for more details.)

Standard would continue to dominate the business and spur growth and improvements in the refining process. Rockefeller's near monopoly of the industry, however, drew ire from competitors and the attention of the government, and in 1911 the U.S. Supreme Court ordered that the Standard empire be broken up into many smaller, independent companies.

Along with the former Standard components, other significant companies would grow and enter the industry, especially with the discovery of significant oil deposits in other regions, including Texas, Oklahoma, Kansas, Wyoming, and California. The chart on page 13 lists the largest oil companies in the United States by the late 1930s.

The discovery of huge oil deposits at Spindletop in Texas in 1901 launched the modern era of the petroleum industry. The first well, known as the "Lucas Gusher" for engineer Anthony F. Lucas, was drilled just south of Beaumont. It hit in spectacular fashion, and was soon producing 100,000 barrels a day (3.6 million bbls in its first year). The well and oil field would lead to the Gulf Coast area becoming established as a center for oil production and refining.

The expanding reach of the automobile created increasing demands for gasoline, and growing consumer and industrial markets for kerosene, lubricating oil, and other products led to increased demand and production. By 1905, total oil production in the U.S. topped 120 million barrels.

Improved refining techniques and railcars

Refining methods improved from the 1880s and later, first by sealing the kettles and using copper condensing tubes to capture fractions as they separated from the crude and evaporated. By the early 1900s, large vertical tower stills were appearing, which allowed multi-stage distillation in batches. This led in the 1910s to fractionating towers that used a continuous distillation process to capture more fractions. Chapter 2 explains the refining process in detail.

Additional products came from these processes. Kerosene would remain a primary product of refining into the 1930s, when electricity reached most

Gasoline use increased dramatically through the 1910s as branded service stations began appearing nationwide. This Skelly station in Nebraska dates to the 1920s; note the open-cab tank delivery truck at right. *History Nebraska collection*

rural areas, eliminating most need for kerosene lamps.

Along with the growth in auto sales in the early 1900s, American involvement in World War I spurred gasoline demand even higher, with a sudden need for large quantities of motor fuels to power vehicles, tanks, planes, and other military equipment. Gasoline production grew from 5 million barrels in 1900 to 16 million barrels in 1910 and 96 million barrels in 1920. In 1919, gasoline replaced kerosene as the most common refined product.

In the 1920s, railroads were the primary method of shipping refined petroleum products, and they carried crude oil to the refineries, as well. Some pipelines were in use, but most carried crude from oil fields to refineries. By this period, tank cars had evolved and grown, with typical capacity of 6,000 to 8,000 gallons.

Most of the 83,000 tank cars in service on U.S. railroads at the time were engaged in carrying oil and oil products; in 1920, they hauled 6.4 million tons of crude oil and 29.9 million tons of product. Virtually all revenue-service tank cars were privately owned, either by petroleum companies or leasing companies. The 13,000

Modern refineries are marked by tall fractionating towers or columns, along with large cracking units and a maze of piping. This TotalEnergies refinery in Port Arthur, Texas, shown in 2014, currently has a capacity of 200,000 barrels per day. *Carol Highsmith, Library of Congress*

During World War II, railroads ran solid trains of oil and gasoline from the Southwest to coastal ports. Here a set of Santa Fe FTs leads an oil train extra freight (white flags on locomotive) out of Cushing, Okla. *Santa Fe*

railroad-owned tank cars were strictly in company service, carrying fuel, oil, and water for steam locomotives and maintenance uses.

Basic railroad operations had evolved to railroads carrying carloads of finished products from refineries to local bulk depots and dealers around the country (more than 16,500 of them by 1926). These dealers then used trucks to make final deliveries to gas stations and other customers.

Oil companies were working to improve gasoline quality to help engine performance. Gasoline in the early 1920s was 40 to 60 octane (compare that to today's 87-octane regular gas). Gas engines were inefficient, low-compression devices. A big problem for engines of the period was "knocking," caused by fuel prematurely firing, which throws an engine out of balance. Severe knocking can damage and crack engine components.

The solution would come in the form of tetraethyl lead (TEL), which increased octane, reduced engine-component wear, and served as an anti-knock agent. The effective agent was the lead component; TEL included solvents that allowed it to be mixed readily with gasoline.

The first "ethyl gasoline" was sold in February 1923. It was extremely successful, increasing octane, eliminating knock, and allowing development of more powerful, higher compression engines.

However, TEL was also extremely hazardous. Seventeen workers died of lead exposure at production plants in the early 1920s, and many others were permanently disabled. Even when production methods were improved and made safer, vehicle exhaust for the next 50 years would leave a toxic coat of lead almost everywhere on the planet. The oil industry did its best to deflect these concerns, and it wasn't until the 1970s that lead would finally be removed from fuel, with other ingredients and processes providing the necessary properties in gasoline.

Modern refining and rail operations

Along with improved distillation methods, refineries continued growing in size and implementing new technologies. These included thermal cracking in 1913 (using heat to break down hydrocarbon molecule strings, allowing more gasoline production)

From the steam through early diesel eras, the 50-ton general-purpose tank car was the standard car for delivering petroleum products. This 8,000-gallon Gulf car, built in 1930 and shown in 1960, was typical; common sizes ranged from 6,000 to 10,000 gallons. *J. David Ingles collection*

In the 1960s, tank car size began growing dramatically as weight limits increased. This 33,000-gallon multi-diameter LPG car was built by ACF in 1964. *J. David Ingles*

and catalytic ("cat") cracking in 1937, which used separate catalysts to crack molecules more efficiently. (See chapter 2 for more on cracking.)

By 1939, there were 435 oil refineries in operation in the U.S., with an average capacity of just over 9,000 barrels of production a day. Most refineries were located near major producing oil fields to limit the distance of crude oil transport, with many in Oklahoma, Texas, Pennsylvania, and along the Gulf coast (with its convenient ocean shipping ports), but there were refineries in many other areas as well. (The map on page 30 in Chapter 2 shows U.S. oil fields and current refinery locations.)

The onset of World War II drove the oil industry to increase production, first as the U.S. provided fuel and materials to Great Britain under the Lend-Lease Act in early 1941, then increasing as the U.S. officially entered the war that December. By war's end, the number of refineries had dropped to 380, but the average capacity of

Early oil fields were a maze of tall derricks at individual wells. "Gushers" like this one, at Spindletop, Texas (this is Heywood well No. 2) in 1901, looked impressive but wasted oil and caused damage. Technology soon evolved to cap wells to contain pressure.
Library of Congress

those that remained had grown to 13,400 bbl/day, and total U.S. refining capacity was 5.08 million bbl/day, an increase of about 1.1 million bbl/day compared to 1939.

A major development during the war was the tremendous expansion of pipelines across the country. The lack of pipeline capacity and the sinking of tanker ships off the East Coast had led to the mobilization of tank cars nationwide, with a coordinated effort among railroads and oil companies to run solid trains of crude oil and refined products to coastal ports (more on that in Chapter 7).

Two major wartime projects were the "Big Inch" and "Little Big Inch" pipelines from the Southwest to the Midwest and East. Following the war, they were privatized and converted to product pipelines. Many other pipelines followed, and oil companies soon had extensive networks serving tank terminals around the country (see Chapter 4).

Largest oil companies, 1938

This table lists the 20 largest oil companies in the U.S., shown by their percentage of total U.S. refining capacity. The top 10 companies accounted for 58.6% of total capacity; the top 20 made up 76.6% of total capacity.

COMPANY (BRAND)	%
1. Standard of New Jersey (Esso)	9.9
2. Socony-Vacuum (Mobil)	8.1
3. Texas Co. (Texaco)	7.5
4. Standard of Indiana (Standard, American)	6.2
5. Standard of California	5.8
6. Shell	5.8
7. Gulf	5.0
8. Consolidated Oil Corp. (Sinclair)	4.8
9. Tidewater (Flying A)	3.0
10. Cities Service	2.5
11. Atlantic	2.5
12. Richfield	2.4
13. Pure	2.2
14. Union of California (Union 76)	2.2
15. Ohio Oil Co. (Marathon)	2.0
16. Sun Oil Co. (Sunoco)	2.0
17. Phillips (Phillips 66)	1.5
18. Standard of Ohio (Sohio, Boron)	1.3
19. Continental (Conoco)	1.0
20. Mid-Continent (DX)	0.9

By the 1940s, walking-beam pumps were common at oil wells. This one is near McPherson, Kan., in 1941. Derricks would soon be used only for drilling and would be removed after the well was producing. *Marion Post Wolcott, Library of Congress*

The growth in pipelines and tank terminals eliminated many rail shipments, as pipelines became responsible for most long-distance transport of products, with final delivery by truck. Railcars still served many of these tank terminals, but with shorter, fewer runs, as increasing capacity of semi-trailers and the growth of interstate highways expanded the practical distance of truck deliveries.

Another postwar development was the growth of natural-gas pipelines, running from oil fields to large cities across the nation. These eliminated the local manufactured-gas (coal gas) plants that had been landmarks in most large urban areas.

The marketing of propane and butane gases, which were previously considered waste products and burned off at refinery flares, began in the late 1920s, usually blended as liquified petroleum gas (LPG). Together with fuel oil, LPG became a common replacement for coal in home heating, especially in small towns and rural areas away from the gas mains (local delivery pipelines) in large urban areas. Railroads became, and remain, a major shipper of LPG across the country.

Today, 129 U.S. refineries process about 18 million bbls/day of crude oil. The industry remains a highly volatile one, with frequent boom and bust cycles depending upon multiple factors including world crude prices and supply levels, domestic demands for various products, new domestic oil discoveries, and continued evolution of well drilling and refining methods.

Oil wells and oil field operations

Getting the oil out of the ground is the first important step in the process. Though the science and process have evolved significantly, drilling oil wells remains tough, dirty work. This description is greatly simplified, but it

Standard Oil monopoly and breakup

The biggest success story in the early oil industry—and in American industrial history—was the formation and growth of the Standard Oil Company. John D. Rockefeller started the company in 1863 (and incorporated it in 1870), just a few years after the first Pennsylvania oil well was tapped. With several associates and partners, Rockefeller had soon created the largest oil company in the world.

Rockefeller's business was an early example of horizontal integration—buying smaller, competing companies to grow your market and business, keeping the ones that were successful, and shutting down those that weren't. Standard was soon the largest company by far in the new industry. By the 1870s and 1880s, Rockefeller and his associates were effectively managing dozens of theoretically separate companies that essentially operated as one under Rockefeller's leadership. Standard's size enabled it to receive rebates and discounts from railroads and other related businesses, giving it a price advantage over its competitors. By 1890, Standard controlled about 90 percent of the U.S. oil market.

Other companies—in other industries as well as oil—were leery of companies becoming monopolies, so in response, Congress passed the Sherman Antitrust Act in 1890. The Act was designed to prevent monopolies by forbidding contracts that restrained trade of other companies. Standard Oil was among the Act's first targets.

The company's response was to become a holding company for the dozens of other companies that it controlled (many of which were, in turn, holding companies for other businesses). But the effect was still the same, in that dozens of companies were controlled by the Standard Trust.

The huge growth in demand for fuel caused by the rise of the automobile after the turn of the century, along with the discovery of significant new oil deposits in Texas and the Southwest (with the formation of many new companies to tap those areas), reduced Standard's market share, but it still controlled 64 percent of the market in 1911.

The situation came to a head in 1909 with a lawsuit filed by the U.S. Justice Department under the Sherman Act charging Standard with "sustaining a monopoly and restraining interstate commerce." A significant part of this was railroad-related, as Standard Oil subsidiary Union Tank Line (UTLX) owned a majority of the tank cars in the U.S. Even though in theory Union operated as a separate company as a lessor of tank cars, it was controlled by Standard and served its interests.

In 1911, the Supreme Court upheld a lower-court decision agreeing that Standard Oil violated the Act; it ordered the dissolution of the company. Specifically, it required Standard be broken into 43 independent companies, each with separate boards of directors.

The major companies formed as a result of the breakup were Standard of Ohio (Sohio), now part of BP; Standard of Indiana (later American/Amoco, now part of Tesoro); Standard of New York (Socony), which later merged with Vacuum and became Mobil, now part of ExxonMobil; Standard of New Jersey (Esso), renamed Exxon, now part of ExxonMobil; Standard of California (Socal), later renamed Chevron, now ChevronTexaco; Atlantic and Richfield, which merged (Arco) and are now part of BP, but with Atlantic operations spun off to Sunoco; Standard of Kentucky (Kyso), later acquired by Socal; and Continental Oil Company (Conoco), now part of ConocoPhillips. This is a very simplified version; many companies have merged and spun off operations and divisions.

Union Tank Line became Union Tank Car Co., and was also spun off as a separate company. It continued its role as a car leasing company, expanding operations and continuing as the largest tank car leasing company through most of the 1900s. It began building its own cars in 1956 and today operates about 120,000 tank cars (including its Canadian subsidiary, Procor).

Small crude oil storage tanks are located near wells or groups of wells. These are near Wichita, Kan., in 1941. Depending on their proximity to refineries, the crude can then travel by pipeline, rail, or truck. *Marion Post Wolcott, Library of Congress*

A large walking-beam pump works in the background, with crude storage tanks at left. Note the electric lines providing power for this Wyoming installation in 2010. Wind socks (the orange cone atop a tank) let workers know safe areas in case of release of hazardous gases. *Jeff Wilson*

A small walking-beam pump works in the foreground as several tank cars are loaded with crude oil near Salem, Ill., about 50 miles east of St. Louis. Wells in the area produced about 200,000 barrels per day when this photo was taken in 1940. *Arthur Rothstein, Library of Congress*

A Baltimore & Ohio Geep switches a crude oil loading rack near Mineral City, Ohio, in 1971. The small oil field, in operation in the 1970s and 1980s, produced about 100 oil loads a month for the railroad. *John E. Beach*

will provide a better understanding of the production process.

Through the early 1900s, a derrick was constructed (later, a portable derrick moved into position) at a site and a hole was drilled vertically to reach the oil deposit. Distances can be significant: Average well depth was around 3,500 feet in the 1940s, and is now close to 6,000 feet.

The drilling process is tedious, involving attaching lengths of pipe together and sending them downward. Drilling bits become dull and must be pulled up, replaced, and the process repeated.

Complicating matters is that the earth overburden that must be drilled through—a mix of topsoil, sand, and clay—is often unstable, and collapses back upon itself in the hole. To control this, water or oil and a controlled mix of solids known as "drilling mud" are injected into the hole, which stabilizes the opening, helps control pressure, lubricates the drill bit, and aids in removal of debris.

Through the 1930s, the tall derricks—which remain an icon in the industry—were a permanent part of the wellhead. Early derricks were wood, changing to steel by the 1930s. These held the vertical pipe, drilling line, and other equipment. The late 1930s saw the growth of portable rigs that could be moved and reused after a well had been drilled and established.

When oil is found, the well is capped to control the pressure. Some deposits are under extreme pressure, and if it's not controlled, a "blowout"—an uncontrolled release of crude oil and gas—can occur. This can destroy equipment, kill and injure workers, and if ignited can be extremely difficult to control. These "gushers" were common at the turn of the 20th century, but improved control devices allowed wells to be more easily capped by the 1920s.

Some wells have enough pressure to keep oil flowing on its own; on others, a separate pump is needed to draw the oil upward. These pumps, although varying in size and specific details, have a common appearance. A gas, diesel, or electric engine or motor turns a crank that moves a walking beam that slowly dips up and down. At the free end is the "horse head," which pulls a sucker rod up from the well pipe, drawing up the oil.

A high-producing oil field may have dozens of these pumps going within view; small fields may have one or two, all producing at different rates.

The oil coming out of the ground isn't ready for the refinery. It's a mix of crude oil, gas, and water, and must be safely separated to capture the oil.

Workers load a crude oil tank car (far left) and three butane cars (right) at the Seminole County oil field in Oklahoma in 1939. The tall platforms provide good access to the cars. *Russell Lee, Library of Congress*

When the crude first comes out of the ground, it passes through a separator. Residual water is separated, collected, and treated. Gases (methane, ethane, propane, butane) will also be collected or burned with a flare. The separated oil is collected at a small tank near the wellhead.

Depending upon the location, number of local wells, and distance from the refinery, the oil is periodically collected by truck and carried to a shipping point, or it travels via a small gathering pipeline (typically 4" in diameter) to a larger gathering tank, which serves multiple wells. From the gathering tank, the crude is then shipped to a refinery, either by pipeline, rail, or truck—again, depending upon the size of the operation, number of wells, total production, and distances involved.

Along with major oil fields, many smaller areas have had oil wells, often in areas that weren't thought of as oil-production areas. Through the 1950s, if it was thought that a few hundred thousand barrels could be squeezed out of the ground, there was probably an investor or company who was willing to try it.

Rail was the common method of transport for these small operations, as it didn't pay to lay a pipeline, and distances to refineries were too far for trucks to be practical. Some of these were regular producers, shipping a handful of tank cars a week until the production became financially impractical.

Fracking and modern oil fields

The early 2000s saw the development of new techniques to get oil from deposits in shale, which earlier had been impractical because the oil and natural gas were trapped within pores in the rock. Called "fracking," the method involves using hydraulic fracturing combined with horizontal drilling.

After boring into the shale, a mix of water, sand (extremely hard, crush-resistant, rounded grains of quartz), and chemicals is injected at high pressure. The pressure cracks the rocks open; the sand particles hold the cracks open enough to allow the oil and gas to release, whereupon it is captured.

Horizontal drilling makes the operation practical, as it allows an entire seam of shale to be worked along its length, as opposed to conventional vertical drilling, where only a small cross-section could be worked with each bore.

Fracking opened up large areas for drilling, mainly for oil in North Dakota's Bakken field and South Texas's Eagle Ford shale field, plus in several natural-gas fields.

Another key area for oil was in northern Alberta's tar sands, a huge deposit of thick oil mixed with sand (called bitumen). The product is so thick that it must either must be mined (like coal) or heated underground to become thin enough to pump to the surface. It requires extensive processing, like residual in a refinery. Bitumen can't be sent through a pipeline unless it's diluted with 28 percent distillate, which creates an issue for the receiving refinery, because the distillate has to be treated and disposed.

Bitumen can be shipped by tank car, but it requires heated, insulated cars to

Drilling mud

Commercial drilling mud (or drilling fluid) became available in the 1940s as multiple companies developed specific products. The Magnet Cove Barium Corporation (Magcobar), formed in 1940, was one such company supplying products that well drillers would mix with oil or water and inject into the well hole. The company had a 200-plus-car fleet of leased boxcars (this one from North American) bearing its logo to carry bagged products.

Magcobar was one of several companies that began supplying drilling mud to oil companies in the 1940s. This insulated plug-door boxcar, leased from North American, was built in 1964 and photographed in the early 1980s. *Jeff Wilson collection*

Crude oil is loaded into tank cars at Musket's Windsor, Colo., terminal on the Great Western Railway in 2013. The terminal could outload 12,000 barrels per day at the time, but was being expanded. *Chip Sherman*

Petroleum industry timeline	
1859	"Drake's Folly": Edwin Drake drills the first commercial U.S. oil well, at Titusville, Pa.
1860s	Tank cars first used to carry crude oil from oil fields to refineries.
1866	Number of refineries grows rapidly; Pittsburgh area has 60 oil refineries.
1870	Standard Oil Company incorporated by John D. Rockefeller.
1890	Standard Oil controls 90 percent of U.S. refining capacity.
1900	U.S. oil production reaches 170,000 barrels a day.
1900	6,800 miles of crude oil pipelines are in service.
1901	Major oil deposits are discovered in Texas (Spindletop).
1910	U.S. gasoline production reaches 16 million barrels.
1911	Supreme Court orders breakup of Standard Oil.
1913	Thermal cracking introduced, allowing increased gasoline production.
1919	Gasoline production exceeds kerosene production.
1920	U.S. gasoline production hits 96 million barrels.
1920	Tank cars carry 6.4 million tons of crude and 29.9 million tons of petroleum products.
1923	Tetraethyl lead is first added to gasoline to boost octane.
1925	Average gasoline octane rating: regular 56, premium 72.
1926	More than 16,000 bulk oil terminals are in business in the U.S.
1937	Catalytic cracking introduced, increasing gasoline output.
1940	Tank cars carry 5 million tons of crude and 55.8 million tons of products.
1943	"Big Inch" and "Little Big Inch" pipelines are completed, easing strain on railroad transports.
1945	380 U.S. refineries in operation; they process 5.1 million barrels of oil per day
1949	Average gasoline octane rating: regular 83, premium 90.
1964	The U.S. has 148,000 miles of crude oil pipelines, 57,000 miles of liquid product pipelines, and 710,000 miles of natural gas pipelines.
1970	The DOT limits tank car size at 34,500 gallons and 263,000 pounds gross rail load (GRL).
1979	Shelf-style couplers are required on new tank cars.
2014	U.S. railroads terminated a record 493,146 carloads of crude oil.
2021	The U.S. has 200,000 miles of liquid petroleum pipelines in service.
2022	129 U.S. refineries in operation, with a total capacity of 18 million barrels/day.
2022	About 443,000 tank cars are in North American service (85,000 high-pressure cars).

move it, and it's generally diluted with 17 percent distillate (creating what's termed "railbit").

Although oil from fracking doesn't present the handling issues of tar sands bitumen, it has presented its own hazards. Bakken oil (a type of light sweet crude) has proven to be extremely volatile and has been involved in multiple explosive accidents involving trains. This provided the impetus that led to improved tank car safety features (see Chapter 5) and the removal of older cars from service.

The lack of crude pipelines in fracking areas, along with the long distances to refineries, led to a tremendous growth in rail crude transports. Unit trains from these fields now carry crude to refineries in many areas of the country, as crude carloadings went from negligible (5,000 carloads in 2006) to significant (234,000 loads by 2012 and growing).

This crude market is subject to considerable fluctuation, and although crude oil rail traffic has slowed in the 2020s, it still remains a key source of business for railroads.

At oil fields that use fracking, the frac sand is delivered by two-bay covered hoppers. This 110-ton, 3,250-cubic-foot car was built by Gunderson in 2014. *Cody Grivno*

Railroads themselves are a major consumer of petroleum products. These UTLX tank cars are delivering diesel fuel to New York, New Haven & Hartford's Dover Street Yard in Boston (storage tank at right). *New Haven*

CHAPTER TWO

Oil refineries

A Norfolk Southern train of crude oil from North Dakota's Bakken oil fields rolls into the loop track to prepare for unloading at the Delaware City, Del., refinery in 2013. The facility, owned by PBF Energy, has a capacity of 210,000 barrels per day. Modern refineries are marked by tall fractionating towers and cracking units. *Michael S. Murray*

Oil refineries evolved from simple distillation stills to large, complex facilities with fractionating towers, cracking units, and other advanced systems. Although railroads' roles in serving refineries have diminished and changed over the past 100 years, railroads still serve refineries by delivering inbound crude oil, catalysts, and additives and hauling out gasoline, LPG, lube oil, and other products.

Crude oil and fractions

Before explaining refineries and the refining process, it's important to understand crude oil, the raw material for all petroleum products. You don't need chemist-level knowledge of carbon molecule structure, but having an understanding of crude oil composition will help you better understand how a refinery works and what it's trying to accomplish.

All crude oil is not the same. Depending upon the oil field, crude oil content varies in levels of paraffins (waxes), aromatics, naphthene, sulfur, and other properties. Another factor is its weight as measured by API (American Petroleum Institute) gravity (the oil's weight/density compared to water). Crude with an API gravity over 10 will float on water ("light" crude); under 10 will sink ("heavy" crude).

Fractions from crude oil

This is a simplified list of the fractions obtained by distilling crude oil. The "C" numbers in parentheses indicate the number of carbon atoms in the molecules of each fraction (there is overlap because of divisions within the fractions).

Gases (C1 to C4)—Methane (lightest), ethane, propane, butane. Methane and ethane make up natural gas; propane and butane are blended as liquified petroleum gas (LPG) and used as fuel and as feedstock for petrochemicals.

Naphthas (C5 to C9)—The lightest liquids; very volatile. They're used as a base for solvents, as cleaning solutions, blended with gasoline, and as a petrochemical feedstock to make other compounds.

Gasoline (C5 to C12)—Blended with naphthas and other additives to increase octane; used as motor fuel. It's the primary product of the refining process.

Kerosene (C12 to C18)—Originally used for lighting and heating; now processed mainly as jet fuel.

Distillates or light oils (C14 to C20)—Blended with additives and marketed as Nos. 1, 2, and 3 fuel oil and diesel fuel.

Heavy oils (C20 to C70)—Processed to make Nos. 4, 5 (Bunker B), and 6 (Bunker C) fuel oils, lubricating oils, and greases; heavy oils are often further cracked and alkylized to make gasoline, diesel fuel, and jet fuel.

Asphalt and VDRs (vacuum distillate residuals, C71 and up)—Solids that won't boil. They are sometimes processed as asphalt and tar; modern refineries send most residuals to a coker, which cracks it to heavy oil, gasoline, and naphtha. The residual product when finished is petroleum coke, or "petcoke."

The batch-process still (center right) at this circa-1907 refinery has a 600-barrel capacity. At left is the boiler/pump house; in the distance between them is a 5,000-barrel crude oil storage tank. The refinery was in Chanute, Kan. *Library of Congress*

Typical of small refineries of the period, this Barnsdall refinery in Wichita, Kan., processed 5,000 barrels per day in the early 1940s. A fractionating tower stands just to the left of the tall sign. *Marion Post Wolcott, Library of Congress*

Sulfur content (or lack thereof) is also important: Crude oil high in sulfur is termed "sour" while low-sulfur oils are "sweet."

These varying properties result in higher and lower yields of specific final products (more or less gasoline or lubricating oil, for example), and refineries often blend crude of different properties before processing it. Crude also varies widely in viscosity and in appearance, from nearly clear to brown, red, or black.

Chemically speaking, crude oil is about 84% carbon, 14% hydrogen, and 1% to 3% sulfur, with traces of other elements. Salts and trace metals must be removed before or during processing.

Crude comprises a mix of hydrocarbon molecules, each of which includes one or more atoms of each (hydrogen and carbon). The refining process breaks those molecules down and separates them, grouping them into separate products called fractions. The fewer the carbon atoms in the molecule, the lighter the fraction: for example, gases have one to four carbon atoms; liquids, five to 70; and solids, 70 or more. For example, propane (C_3H_8) has three carbon atoms and eight hydrogen atoms and is a gas at normal atmospheric pressure.

The first primitive refining processes of the 1860s focused on kerosene; later came gasoline and lubricating oils, and by the early 1900s, various refinery processes allowed virtually all of the crude oil to be processed.

Each gas, liquid, or solid fraction has unique properties and various end-product uses. The chart on page 23 lists the common fractions, along with their carbon counts from lightest to heaviest, and includes some typical uses. The lighter the fraction, the more volatile (the more quickly it will evaporate).

Workers make adjustments at the base of a small fractionating tower at an Oklahoma refinery in 1939. *Russell Lee, Library of Congress*

Early refineries

Refining is the process of distilling crude to capture its fractions. The descriptions that follow cover refineries in general, but no two refineries are exactly the same. Most are designed to capture as much gasoline as possible, but other refineries are designed to specialize in other products, such as lubricating oil.

The most basic way to refine crude oil is by applying heat. As the temperature of the oil rises, the lightest fractions rise to the surface and evaporate or are captured. The first refineries of the early 1860s were simple stills that heated kettles of crude oil over an open fire (known as "atmospheric distillation"). The gas fractions were simply allowed to evaporate, while the next fractions—naphtha, gasoline, and kerosene—were literally skimmed off the top. At the time, kerosene was the most desired fraction, in demand for use in lamps and lighting. Most other products, including gasoline, were considered waste products and were burned off or otherwise discarded.

As you can imagine, this method was inefficient, slow, messy, and above all, dangerous. Fires and explosions were common. As demand for kerosene and other products increased, safer and more efficient distillation methods were needed.

The first step was to cover the container being heated, with a coiled copper condensing pipe at the top. This allowed collecting the fractions as they gassed off, then directing them downward and away from the heat

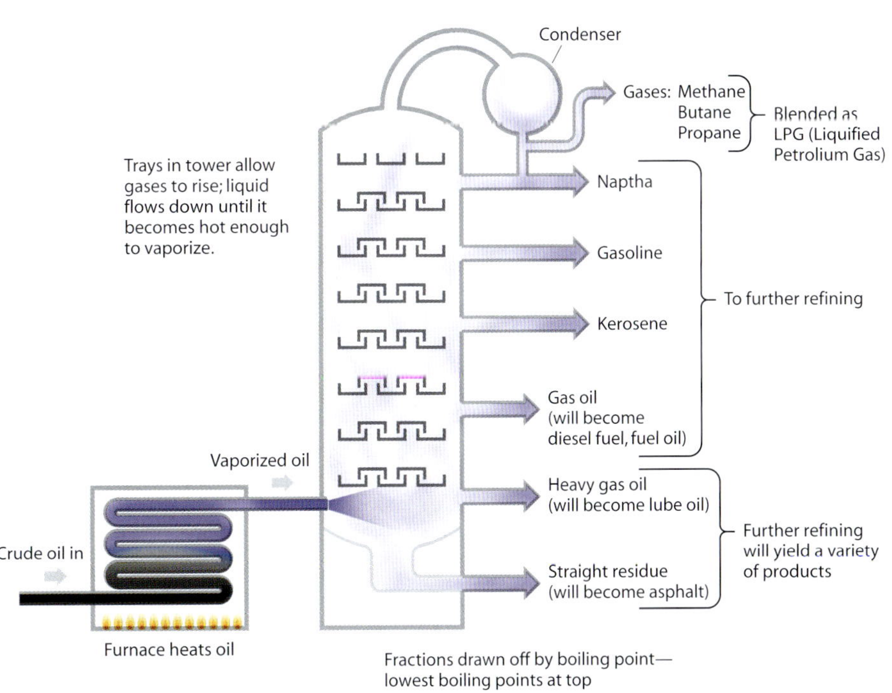

Fractions from a barrel (42 gallons) of crude oil

Average fractions; exact amounts vary by composition of crude oil, era, and refinery methods

Gasoline (46%)
19.4 gallons

Diesel and fuel oils (25%)
10.5 gallons

Jet fuel/kerosene (10%)
4.1 gallons

Heavy fuel and lube oils (4%)
1.7 gallons

Propane, butane (3.5%)
1.5 gallons

Asphalt and residuals (3%)
1.3 gallons

Petroleum feedstock (2.5%)
1.1 gallons

Napthas, other products (6%)
2.4 gallons

Several tank cars rest on the cleaning track at the Humble refinery in Baytown, Texas, in December 1944. The tall structure is a catalytic cracker. Steam is rising from the cleaning hoses in the tank cars. As the runoff on the ground shows, the environment was not a priority for early refineries. *Standard Oil Co.*

The dewaxing unit stands prominently above the Mid-Continent refinery in Tulsa, Okla., in 1943. *John Vachon, Library of Congress*

source, where they could cool and condense back to liquid.

As refining technology and methods improved, multiple large furnaces heated bigger, taller stills that processed larger batches of oil. (A photo of an early refinery is shown on pages 8-9 in Chapter 1). Early oil refining batch processes, however, were not efficient, and these early refineries were a huge source of air and ground pollution.

Fractionating towers

The first major step toward modern refining was the fractionating tower, which allowed a continuous process called "fractional distillation" that was more efficient compared to the older, smaller batch-process stills. These began appearing around 1920 and quickly became the standard refining method.

A drawing of a fractionating tower is shown on page 25. The basic operating principle is simple. A continuous run of crude oil is pumped through a coiled pipe and heated using steam from a furnace at the base of the tower. The steam, at more than 1,100° F, vaporizes the incoming crude, which is then injected into the lower part of the fractionating tower.

Inside the tower are a series of collection trays at varying heights, with multiple openings in each tray to allow vapor to rise. These openings have cap-shaped covers ("bubble caps") over them to slow the rise of the vapors. As the vaporized oil enters the tower—which is hotter at the bottom than the top—the vapor rises until it condenses back to a liquid. This liquid then flows into a tray just below it. The trays at each level capture the liquids (the separated fractions) and route them within the refinery.

Individual fractions are thus separated as the vapor rises to a point where the temperature in the tower matches that fraction's boiling point, whereupon it condenses to liquid. Thus, the lighter the fraction (and the lower its boiling point), the higher it rises in the tower before turning into a liquid and settling in a tray. Gases pass through all trays through the top of the tower, where they are captured by the condenser. The heaviest fractions (residuals) are collected from the base of the tower for further processing.

The fractionating tower is efficient and works well. Most refineries were soon installing multiple towers to process crude oil, continuing the trend toward larger refineries. Towers vary in size by capacity, with most from 18 to

The Colonial Beacon (Beacon Oil Co.) refinery in Everett, Mass., covered about 100 acres and processed 15,000 barrels a day in 1948. The refinery received its crude by ships on the Mystic River. The tank car loading racks are in the middle, between the refinery itself (lower left) and storage tanks (top and upper right). *Jeff Wilson collection*

U.S. oil fields and refineries

Red dot = Refinery
Black dot = City
Refineries are as of 2022;
Oil fields are areas that have produced crude oil since 1870.

Pressure tanks have hemispherical ends; some are spheres (backround middle). They are used to store liquified gases. This is the Phillips refinery at Borger, Texas, in the early 1940s. *Library of Congress*

25 feet in diameter and some as tall as 80 feet.

The fractions are then each further processed, treated, purified, and blended (with other fractions or outside additives) to produce final products.

Cracking, coking, blending

The diagram on page 26 shows the average percentage of various products that result when crude is run through a fractionating tower. The exact percentages vary depending upon the properties and makeup of the incoming crude (which is why refineries often blend it before refining) and by the era and technology used in refining.

By the early 1900s, gasoline was becoming the most desired product, so oil companies looked for methods that would produce a higher percentage of it. Being able to alter other fractions gives refineries flexibility in adjusting refinery output based on demand and need for products instead of "straight-run" products (the direct products of initial distillation).

Typical refinery output, 1949

Since there's no such thing as a truly "typical" refinery, this chart shows a realistic output for a steam- or early diesel-era 10,000 bbl/day refinery, representing a capacity just below the average for its day. Keep in mind that not all finished products would necessarily be shipped by rail.

PRODUCT	% OF TOTAL OUTPUT	OUTPUT IN GALLONS	TANK CARS
Gasoline	40	168,000	21
Diesel/fuel oil/lube oil	22	92,400	12
Kerosene	8	33,600	2
Naphtha*	5	21,000	2
LPG (propane, butane)*	7	29,400	3
Asphalt**	3	12,600	2
Residuals**	15	63,000	—

* Naphtha would be blended with other products; some LPG is used as fuel in refinery.

** Would often be cracked to make other products as desired, usually increasing gasoline output.

1 barrel (bbl) = 42 gallons

Estimates are based on 8,000-gallon tank cars for liquids and 11,000-gallon cars for LPG

Flares burn off waste gases and gases from unsafe pressure buildup throughout the refinery system. This is the Cenex (CHS) refinery in Laurel, Mont., in 2009. *Jeff Wilson*

Flares may be large, with multiple outlets in a single fixture. The tops of these multi-nozzle flares at an Exxon refinery in Baytown, Texas, in the 1970s, stand 300 feet above ground level. *Jeff Wilson collection*

The first solution was "cracking," a process that breaks down the heavy fractions and residuals (those with long strings of carbon atoms in their molecules) into smaller ones. The first method of doing this, used beginning in 1913, was thermal cracking. This method uses extreme heat and pressure (up to 1,400° F and 1,000 psi) to physically break up the molecules of these heavy products; the result is light mid-level distillates, including naphtha, gasoline, and diesel fuel (which would increase greatly in demand by the 1930s).

When the lighter products have been cracked, heavy residual is left over. This can be processed into asphalt or tar or marketed as what was known as "bunker fuel." "Bunker C," or No. 6 fuel oil, was a common fuel for oil-fired steam locomotives and early gas-electric-turbine locomotives. It required heating to around 200° to flow easily enough for use. Its primary advantage was that it was cheap.

Another early refining process is coking, first used in 1932. It's a form of thermal cracking that yields light fractions and produces as a residual petroleum coke, or "petcoke." Like coke made from coal, petcoke has many industrial uses.

Although thermal cracking works well, the process takes a great deal of heat and energy. The cracking units were also subject to rapid wear and stress from the heat and pressure involved. Another concern was octane

Rail loading facilities are key features of refineries. Their size and style vary widely by refinery capacity and era. This small refinery in the early 1900s has two tracks between a tank car loading platform (note the hinged wooden platform with chains) and a warehouse, used for shipping packaged products. *Jeff Wilson collection*

in the gasoline produced (explained in Chapter 1), which would become even more critical as gasoline engines increased in compression and power.

The solution was catalytic ("cat") cracking, first used in 1937. This process uses catalysts and heat (but lower heat and duration) to break heavy molecules into lighter fractions. Catalysts—chemicals that facilitate a chemical reaction but are themselves not changed by the reaction—include bauxite, aluminum hydrosilicate, and silica-alumina.

Cat cracking was more efficient than thermal cracking and resulted in higher yields and more desirable characteristics. The process replaced most thermal operations, although some thermal cracking continued.

Another variation is hydrocracking, first used around 1960. This is a type of cat cracking that takes heavy oils and cracks them into gasoline, diesel, and jet fuel (kerosene).

Other processes are used to combine or alter molecules to produce additional products. An example is alkylation (using sulfuric acid and hydrofluoric acid as catalysts), by which light compounds are blended to form high-octane hydrocarbons, which are then blended with gasoline to increase its octane.

These are just a few of the major refinery processes, but there are many

A worker loads a tank car with gasoline at a refinery in the early 1940s. The 2 x 12 plank used for access would not make the grade for today's OSHA-compliant facilities. This tank car has an older-style screw-on manway hatch. *Library of Congress*

Loading pressure cars with liquified petroleum gas (LPG) requires connecting three lines: two for product and one as a vent (toward the side of the car). This is a Phillips refinery during World War II. *Library of Congress*

The Mid-Continent refinery in Tulsa, Okla., had multiple loading tracks and platforms in this 1942 view. The platforms are supported by steel I-beams. *John Vachon, Library of Congress*

Several tank cars are spotted along the loading platform at the Kerr-McGee refinery at Wynnewood, Okla., in 1980. Fire extinguishers and equipment are red; the platform is painted silver. The tanks at left store LPG. Chain-link fencing with barbed wire or razor wire is standard around the perimeter at refineries. *Andy Sperandeo*

others used to boost octane, lower the viscosity of oils, improve their resistance to breakdown, reduce sulfur content, remove waxes (and other residual solids), remove water, and otherwise improve the quality of fuels, lube oil, and other products.

Most fractions require additional processing to make them useable. "Blending," the last step in refining, is the process that does this. As an example, lubricating and motor oils are made with a tremendous variety of properties and adjusted for weight, viscosity, resistance to thermal breakdown, flash point, and other characteristics.

Another example is gasoline, which is made in various grades and octane ratings. From the 1920s to the 1970s, tetraethlyl lead was added to motor fuel as an octane booster (it's still used in some types of aviation fuel). Naphthas, detergents, and other additives are also used; gasoline is sometimes blended with ethanol just before delivery in a process called "splash blending."

Natural gas, LPG

Although the petroleum gases—methane, ethane, propane, and butane—have similar properties, they are not the same product, and they are treated and marketed differently, usually as "natural gas" and "liquefied petroleum gas" (LPG).

Natural gas is mainly methane with some ethane. It occurs naturally and is a primary product from many wells, and it's also processed at refineries. Compressing natural gas to a liquid requires extremely high pressure or low temperature (-260° F), making it difficult and expensive to transport. It was largely regarded as a waste material until the 1920s, when pipelines made it practical to transport long distances as a gas. By the 1950s, it had largely superseded manufactured gas (coal gas) in urban areas, and is now widely used for home heating and appliances as well as industrial applications and power generation. Because of its properties, it is not transported by rail.

Propane and butane have similar properties. Propane has a flash point of -155° F and a boiling point of -44° F; butane has a flash point of -76° F and boiling point of 30° F. They differ from natural gas in that both can be compressed to a liquid at fairly low pressure (around 100 psi), making it practical to transport them as a liquid by rail and truck, though generally not by pipeline. Like natural gas, propane and butane were considered waste until the late 1920s, when the development of welded, high-pressure tanks made it practical to store and ship.

Propane and butane are sometimes sold independently, but are often blended in varying proportions and sold as LPG. The proportion of the blend depends upon the intended use (heating fuel, propellant, welding, industrial use, or feedstock for other products). As a fuel for home heating, the propane/butane mix is adjusted for seasons (more propane in winter, less in summer) to keep storage pressures even during fluctuations in outdoor temperature.

One characteristic difference between natural gas and LPG is that LPG has a higher energy value, which is why gas appliances require separate settings for each. Liquefied petroleum gas is also heavier than air, while natural gas is lighter than air. This means that spills or leaks of natural gas will dissipate quickly into the air, while LPG can sink and pool in low areas, creating an explosion hazard.

Both gases are naturally odorless, so both commonly have an odorant added to help identify leaks. Some LPG destined for industrial use as a feedstock is non-odorized; railcars carrying it will be stenciled as such. Chapter 6 covers the high-pressure tank cars that carry LPG.

A tanker transport semi is loaded at a refinery during World War II. During the war, tank cars were pulled from most domestic delivery routes and assigned to long-distance hauls connecting refineries with coastal ports. Tank trucks took over most delivery from refineries to fuel wholesalers. *Library of Congress*

Petrochemical industry

The 1950s saw the dramatic rise of the petrochemical industry. Advanced refining and processing methods allowed making synthetic derivatives of many chemicals and materials. Previously low-value residuals at oil refineries were suddenly in high demand as feedstock for these new products, along with naphtha, heavy oils, and LPG. A short list of products coming from this then-new industry include many types of plastic, a variety of polyester textiles and materials, nylon, isopropyl alcohol, synthetic toluene, and butadiene (used to make synthetic rubber).

There's a lot of crossover between the petrochemical industry and oil refining. Refineries ship (often by

The area in and around Port Arthur, Texas, is packed with refineries and tank terminals. Tank cars rest in the foreground with tanks, fractionating towers, and cracking units in the background in 2014. A flare is lit at far left. *Carol M. Highsmith, Library of Congress*

Refineries usually have their own locomotives to move cars within the facility. This center-cab, twin-engine Plymouth CR8 diesel served the Sohio (Standard Oil of Ohio) refinery at Lima, Ohio, through the 1970s. *Louis A. Marre collection*

rail) many products and refining byproducts to petrochemical plants, including propane, butane, naphtha, ethylene, propylene, benzene, petroleum coke, and ammonia. Outbound loads include covered hoppers of plastic and nylon pellets (for injection molding), antifreeze, polyester and plastic films, fibers, and other materials.

Railroads carry many of these products, but space precludes going into great detail because of the specialized nature of many chemicals and acids. Until the 1940s, almost all tank cars carried petroleum products; since then, the petrochemical industry has been responsible for the development of dozens of highly specialized tank car types to carry a wide variety of products.

Size, type, and ownership

Most refineries are located near producing oil fields, with nearby access to crude oil. However, the expansion of crude pipelines in the early 1900s led to construction of refineries in many locations, including decidedly non-oil-territory places such as Chicago (three in the area), Minneapolis, and Duluth. The map on page 30 shows refinery locations as of early 2023, and shows oil fields as well.

Most refineries produce a wide variety of finished products, but some refineries specialize in certain products—motor and lubricating oil, for example. Refineries regularly trade and sell products and fractions among themselves to meet current production needs.

Refinery size is rated on how many barrels of oil the refinery can process in a day. By the mid-1940s, there were 380 refineries in operation in the U.S., with an average capacity of 13,300 barrels (bbls) per day (the total U.S. capacity was 5.1 million bbls/day). As technologies improved and the efficiencies of larger operations became more efficient, the number of refineries dropped, but they became larger. By 1980, there were still 300 U.S. refineries, with an average capacity of 59,600 bbls/day.

The following two decades saw a dramatic drop in the number of refineries, as small, less efficient operations were shut down. By 2000, there were 158 refineries averaging 104,000 bbls/day (total U.S. capacity, 16.5 million bbls/day). As of early 2023, there were 129 refineries left (although, at the time, five were idle); their average capacity was 139,500 bbls/day, with a total capacity of 18 million bbls/day.

Most refineries have historically been owned by specific oil companies, but many are independent. Large companies have multiple refineries, some in foreign countries. Smaller oil companies may own a single refinery and also buy products from other refineries. Refineries are often included

Refineries on ocean or river ports ship products and receive crude and blending oil by ship. Here the then-new ECOL Ltd. refinery in Garyville, La., receives its first tanker of imported crude oil in August 1976. The ship is the *Shell Nacella*, bringing in 600,000 barrels of oil. The refinery had a 200,000 barrel per day capacity. *Jeff Wilson collection*

when companies merge, but they can also be sold off to other companies or independent producers.

Refinery details

Oil refineries are incredibly complex, which is what makes them fascinating to see and to model. Since the 1920s, the most prominent structures are the fractionating towers, which stand above most other equipment. Their specific size varies by capacity, and most refineries have multiple towers.

Cracking units and cokers also have a distinctive appearance, with ladders and access platforms throughout.

Flares are a prominent detail at any refinery. These are tall, narrow pipes used to burn off waste products as they are produced or to release potentially dangerous pressure buildups within pipes and systems. Burning these gases is preferred to simply releasing a potentially hazardous or flammable gas directly into the atmosphere.

Flares vary in size, but top of a flare (seen in the photo on page 35) may have multiple nozzles coming from several sources. Into the 1960s, it wasn't unusual to see flares burning continually at refineries; since that time, improved methods of capturing gases mean flares are only lit when needed.

Refineries require a great deal of tank storage. These are large compared to those you'll find at local fuel dealers. The tank farm area at a refinery will be arranged by type: crude oil storage, tanks for finished products awaiting shipment, and storage for fuel additives, catalysts, and other liquids and gases. All tanks holding hazardous materials require containment dikes, so tank spacing is wide enough to allow this. (Chapter 4, which covers tank terminals, has more details on tank construction, sizing, and details).

Everything in a refinery is connected by a maze of pipes, with valves and other details seemingly everywhere. It would take a petroleum engineer to determine where all are going to and from, but modelers often opt to just capture the overall appearance of these details.

Structures at a refinery include warehouses, maintenance buildings, processing and packaging buildings, and offices. These will vary in size and capacity by the types of products produced. Refineries have on-site firefighting equipment, as well.

How a refinery receives crude oil and how it ships finished products varies by era, refinery, and location (inland or at a port). Most refineries receive all or part of their crude oil by pipeline. This can be from local wells, distant oil fields, or ports. Ships deliver crude to refineries at port locations. Crude may arrive by rail as well; such traffic grew significantly in the early 2000s, as Chapter 7 explains. Crude is then stored in tanks until needed.

The late 1960s saw production of several styles of jumbo tank cars, including these 38,000-gallon, six-axle cars built by ACF for Mobil. The company used them for shipping blending oils from Mobil's Paulsboro, N.J., refinery (shown here) to two other refineries for producing lube oil. *Mobil Oil Corp.*

Refineries will have a significant space for truck loading of both liquid and packaged products, and there will also be a lot for employee parking. The entire complex is surrounded by fencing (chain-link topped by barbed wire or razor wire is common), with a guard shack at the entrance and gates where people, vehicles, and railroad tracks enter.

Refinery-owned vehicles will be throughout the complex, along with maintenance and security workers. Other details can include stacks of pipes, valves, and other components, and stacks of 55-gallon drums and other containers.

The overall appearance of a refinery—whether it looks clean and well maintained or grimy and dirty—will vary by era, size, and the general health of the owning company. Early refineries often had a grimy, oily appearance, especially in the years before extensive pollution standards, controls, and regulations took effect in the 1970s.

Safety is a higher priority since that time, as well. Wood planks laid from loading platforms to tank car platforms have been replaced by fold-down platforms with safety railings. Let prototype photos be your guide.

Use prototype photos as guides for signs, as well. Some oil-company-owned refineries carry large corporate logos, either as stand-alone signs or on buildings and tanks. Other signs are throughout the complex ("No Smoking," "flammable," "inflammable," and other safety warnings dominate), along with directions at loading docks and office buildings.

Rail operations

Railroads were the primary method of shipping products from refineries into the 1940s, so early refineries in particular—even small ones—will host significant rail operations. Even by the 1960s and later, when pipelines were taking over most product shipping, railroads still carry some in- and outbound traffic, so even modern refineries still have tracks and see regular service.

Tracks are often concentrated in one area of the plant, either parallel to the main track serving the refinery or perpendicular to it, with tracks curving to enter the refinery area. Tracks will generally be divided by their purpose: loading gasoline and other liquids; loading LPG; unloading crude oil and other inbound loads (such as tetraethyl lead); loading non-bulk products (including 55-gallon drums and packaged, cased products); and unloading inbound supplies (packaging, empty drums, refinery parts, and other equipment).

Refineries may have a storage/sorting yard either within or adjacent to the refinery complex itself, where deliveries and pickups are made. Since the 1990s it has also become more common for refineries to store products in tank cars and hold them in their own yard until they're shipped.

The vast majority of traffic at a refinery will be tank cars, but there

Along with bulk shipments, refineries ship products packaged and cased (the cardboard cartons of Silver Shell motor oil in this 1940s view) and in other containers (the 55-gallon drums in the background). Oil companies sometimes ship bulk products to separate locations to do packaging. *Jeff Wilson collection*

will be boxcars for cases and drums, gondolas or flatcars for pipe and machinery, and hoppers or covered hoppers for in- and outbound loads of petcoke, catalysts, and other solids. The more modern the facility, the more likely that non-bulk items will travel by truck.

Another key location to model is a cleanout track, where inbound empty tank cars are cleaned and readied for their next loads. Since the 1970s, this means cars are parked above catch basins that capture liquid spills and cleaning fluids to avoid ground contamination. This was not a concern in earlier times, as the photo of tank cars on the cleaning track on page 26 shows.

Most modern refineries are large enough operations that the trains that serve them won't do individual car spotting; instead, they drop off and pick up large cuts of cars. The refinery will have its own switching locomotive or car-moving vehicle, such as a Trackmobile, to move cars as needed.

Track entrances are gated and locked, so security personnel must open them to allow access for switch crews.

MODELING TIPS

It would be difficult to model a complete refinery to scale—even a smaller one of the "classic" era—so some selective compression will be necessary. Since rail operations are usually concentrated in one area, start with modeling the tracks, loading/unloading platforms, and associated piping and details. If room allows, you can add refinery details such as tanks, fractionating towers, and piping.

Walthers has offered kit for a refinery in HO that is rather basic but includes a fractionating tower with furnace and other details; additional piping is available as a separate kit. Vollmer has also offered a refinery kit in HO. Plastruct has produced refinery kits in HO, N, and O scales, and offers a tremendous variety of piping, valves, tanks, and other components. Tanks are available from Walthers and many other manufacturers.

A number of individuals and companies now offer individual components and complete refinery kits in 3-D printed versions in several scales. See turbosquid.com, shapeways.com, and others for what's available.

Another technique is to use photos showing tanks and towers on the backdrop, along with physically modeling the rail facilities and enough piping and 3-D details to allow blending them together. This allows modeling in a fairly limited space, such as along a shelf.

Be sure to keep your modeling era in mind, especially when selecting details like vehicles and railcars. Having period-appropriate tank trucks (Chapter 8) and tank cars (chapters 5 and 6) goes a long way toward creating a realistic setting. Also, remember that tank cars were owned or leased by particular companies, so they should match their refineries. For example, a Texaco refinery would not have Sinclair tank cars parked at the outbound loading racks.

CHAPTER THREE

Petroleum dealers and jobbers

This Pure Oil bulk dealer stood along the Chicago & North Western on the north side of Racine, Wis., in 1955. The land was owned by the railroad and leased to the jobber. The vertical storage tanks are at left; the truck loading platform and a pump for filling the owner's vehicles are at center, and a gas station sign leans against the warehouse at right, where packaged items and barrels were stored. *Bob Johnson; Keith Kohlmann collection*

The bulk oil dealer, or "jobber," is responsible for getting gasoline and other petroleum products from large distributors (refineries and pipeline terminals) and providing the final distribution to gas stations, homes, and other end users. Into the 1960s these small dealers were usually served by rail, and their compact size makes them ideal modeling subjects.

Into the 1900s, dealers used teams of horses pulling tank wagons to make deliveries to stores and homes. Kerosene was the primary product shipped by rail until auto traffic grew in the 1910s and later. *Standard Oil, James Grant Williams; Mont Switzer collection*

The expansion of pipeline networks, the increased size of tank truck trailers, and better highways pushed railroads out of the picture for most bulk dealers by the 1970s, but a few of the larger businesses still remain rail served.

Liquefied petroleum gas (LPG) terminals and dealers began appearing in the 1930s, and since LPG rarely travels by pipeline, railroads still carry much of that traffic. Many dealers today still receive LPG tank cars by rail.

Let's take a look at the evolution of these dealers, their details, how they operated, how railroads served them, and how they fit into the petroleum distribution chain.

Early fuel depots

In the late 1800s, the primary product from refineries was kerosene, used mainly for lighting (replacing whale oil) and sometimes for heating. The rapid growth in the popularity of the automobile at the turn of the 20th century required refining companies to get more gasoline from the crude, and by 1919 motor fuel production topped that of kerosene. At the turn of the 20th century, to obtain either fuel, customers usually had to go to a hardware or general store to buy it; lumberyards and coal dealers sometimes sold it, as well.

The first gas pump appeared in 1898, but it wasn't until just before 1910 that the first dedicated gas stations began appearing. They quickly became popular, and the drive-in "filling station" soon became the common way for motorists to fuel their vehicles. More than 15,000 were in business in the U.S. by 1920, and 100,000 by 1930.

By the mid-1920s, most of these stations were offering other automotive services, such as oil changes, lubrication, and repairs, becoming "service stations." By the late 1930s, larger operations on major highways began catering to the growing trucking business, giving birth to the "truck stop," which often had an attached restaurant or diner.

The growth of the gas station spurred the business of fuel wholesalers—fuel depots or dealers known as "jobbers," who purchased fuel in bulk (usually by the tank car) from a refinery, stored it on-site in large tanks, and used trucks to deliver it to gas stations and other customers such as farms and industries. These jobbers also delivered home heating fuel as coal began giving way to fuel oil for furnaces; they carried lubricating oil

Some jobbers had a gas station at the location of their storage tanks. The rail spur ran behind the tanks at this Scottsbluff, Neb., co-op dealer in 1941. *Marion Post Wolcott, Library of Congress*

and grease (bulk and packaged), diesel, kerosene, and other products required by vehicles and businesses, as well.

In the industry's beginnings, it was not uncommon for a dealer to load his horse-drawn tank wagons or trucks directly from a tank car parked on a spur. These were generally very short-lived; successful dealers soon built permanent tanks.

By 1926 there were 16,500 fuel wholesalers across the country; this number would grow to 30,000 by 1940. Since roads of the period were still largely gravel and dirt, and truck capacity was low (see Chapter 8 for details on fuel trucks), most dealers typically handled small areas. Most small towns had at least one dealer, and large towns might have three, four, or more jobbers. Most exclusively sold petroleum products, but some coal dealers recognized the trend that was coming and added liquid fuels to their product lines. Farm cooperatives also sometimes sold fuel along with their usual feed, fertilizer, and grain.

Through the 1910s, gasoline was usually sold as a generic product, but by the 1920s, gasoline was being marketed by brand. Colorful, recognizable logos and catch phrases, touting the benefits of "That Good Gulf Gasoline" or to "Be Sure With Pure" became common, along with roadside billboards announcing distances to the next gas stations for different brands. Stations offered free road maps (with logos and information) and sold branded packaged products such as motor oil. By the 1930s, about 85 percent of jobbers were branded, as well, with ties to one oil company or refinery. The remainder were independent, seeking the best deals possible.

In many towns and areas, a jobber could own one or more gas stations (and the dealership may be located at a gas station, with adjacent storage tanks); other jobbers had contracts and working relationships with stations under the brand parent company. Gas stations could be company owned or owned locally by individuals with working arrangements and licenses with a specific brand.

Delivering fuel to these dealers and jobbers was almost exclusively the job of railroads through the 1930s. Tank cars carried gasoline, fuel oil, heating oil, kersene, and diesel, while boxcars carried packaged products (such as cases of motor oil) and could bring in drums of lube and motor oil or grease.

Because of this, through the 1950s, petroleum dealers were almost exclusively located directly next to railroad tracks. In fact, the land was often owned by the railroad and leased to the jobber for a good rate, as long as deliveries kept coming in by rail (this is why multiple jobbers were often located together along a common rail spur).

Fuel dealers' sizes and capacities varied widely, but their basic components remained the same. There were storage tanks, unloading pipes or racks for tank cars, a loading rack for trucks, a pump house, and usually

This large 1940s-era Pure dealer has four horizontal storage tanks (note the worker on the catwalk above them) along with several larger vertical tanks. A truck is being loaded at the rack in front of the tanks. *Jeff Wilson collection*

a small building with an office and a warehouse area for products like barrels of lube or motor oil, boxes of canned motor oil, signs, gas pumps, and tools. There was also a lot to park delivery trucks and service vehicles.

Let's look at the individual components, then examine operations.

Storage tanks

The storage tanks are the most visible part of the facility. Tanks are grouped together, and can be placed vertically on the ground or horizontally atop piers or saddles to elevate them (some dealers had both). Tank saddles were often concrete, with hardwood planks between the saddle and tank, but saddles could be steel truss or framework. A rule of thumb for horizontal tanks is that their length usually does not exceed six times their diameter. Their sizes are smaller than those in tank farms (Chapter 4), but the formula in that chapter for determining tank size still applies. Common capacity for individual tanks

Neighboring Texaco and Shell jobbers are still both served by rail in this early 1970s view. Note the many barrel racks and horizontal tank at the Texaco dealer, as well as the forklift, piping, steps/catwalks, concrete containment dikes, warehouses, and other details. *Jeff Wilson collection*

Several tank cars are spotted at a Pure dealer (also shown on page 40). The near tank car, a UTLX class X, is being unloaded—note the pipe from the rack that's been lowered into the manway atop the dome. The pump house is immediately to the left of the car. *Bob Johnson; Keith Kohlmann collection*

MODELING TIPS

Fuel dealers are an ideal modeling subject, especially on any layout set into the 1960s (later for LPG). They are compact, provide frequent operating movements, and are colorful and varied, with recognizable signs and many details out in the open. They are appropriate for any area of the country and along any railroad. They provide a nice relief from industries housed in bland structures.

When modeling depots, keep in mind the era. The older the era, the smaller a depot can be and still be rail served; the later the era, the larger the facility and the less likely it is served by rail. Safety considerations are key at later facilities, with modernized loading racks and handrails and spill containment pans.

Keep car types appropriate. Non-pressure cars carry gasoline and fuel oil; high-pressure cars carry LPG. Make sure cars are also appropriate for the era you're modeling. In general, car size increased from the steam era through today. Chapters 5 and 6 provide lots of details on fuel-service tank cars.

Simpson Oil Co. in Sikeston, Mo., was a Barnsdall station and dealer in 1940. *John Vachon, Library of Congress*

ranged from 8,000-14,000 gallons (in photos, compare their sizes to inbound tank cars to make an educated guess). Individual tanks may have multiple compartments: look for multiple pipe connections and access hatches, and for rivet lines marking the locations of internal dividers.

Some dealers used underground storage tanks, but concerns with tanks rusting and leaking limited their use. A large underground tank can leak slowly for a long time unnoticed, whereas with an above-ground, elevated tank, even a small leak will quickly become apparent.

Tanks were typically riveted steel construction with radial courses, although welded tanks became more common by the 1950s and later. Tanks were usually painted white or silver to better reflect sunlight and dissipate heat, although some were painted dark colors.

Pipe connections at top and bottom connected each tank to the pumphouse for loading and unloading. There was generally a walkway or platform across the tops of the tanks with a ladder or steps for access. An opening or manway at the top allowed checking levels, often done with a long wooden stick painted with graduated lines and numbers.

Some dealers are equipped to unload tank cars from their bottom outlets. In this 1930s scene, a worker has removed the outlet cap (hanging by chain at right) and has connected the flexible hose, which connects to a permanent trackside pipe. Opening the valve will start the flow. *Jeff Wilson collection*

The number of tanks, their sizes, and what they're used for depends upon the amount and type of business done by each dealer. Does that dealer serve more gas stations, industrial customers, or farms? Does he serve many homes and businesses that use fuel oil furnaces? There will be multiple tanks for gasoline (generally two grades, with more capacity for regular than premium), diesel fuel, heating oil, and possibly kerosene.

Several cars are being unloaded via bottom outlets at a gasoline distributor in 2007. The car is an insulated DOT 111A100W1 car buit by ACF in 1991. The top hatch is propped open to allow ventilation while unloading. *Jeff Wilson*

Rail spurs from oil and LPG dealers will have a derail between the mainline connection and loading area, keeping stray cars from rolling and fouling a main track. *Jeff Wilson*

Containment dikes (see Chapter 4) were common for large storage tanks at refineries and tank farms in the early 1900s, but they weren't as common at small dealers until the 1950s. They could be concrete or earth, and styles, usage, and applications varied widely.

Rail operations

Getting fuel from tank cars to storage tanks could be accomplished in a couple of ways. Depots were set up to unload tank cars either from the top or bottom (some had equipment to do both). At a bottom-unloading facility, pipes would run to trackside where tank cars were spotted. These pipes (which were color-coded for various products to prevent cross-contamination) would be connected to the bottom outlets of tank cars via flexible piping or hoses. The outlet valve on the tank car would then be opened (and the hatch opened to provide venting), and the product would travel through the pipe to the pumphouse, which would direct it to the proper storage tank.

At a top-unloading facility, a standpipe stood at trackside, usually with a ladder and access platform. A hose from the standpipe is connected either to the car's top eduction pipe (which extends down into the tank to its floor) or to a flexible pipe or hose that is inserted through the hatch and lowered to the bottom of the tank. The fuel is then pumped to a storage tank.

Most small facilities were set up to unload single cars, so it was important to spot them accurately at the unloading pipes. Larger depots could receive multiple cars at once, so cars could be placed at multiple locations on the spur track.

The rail spur itself may serve just the fuel depot, or it could continue to serve other adjacent businesses (often other fuel depots). The track was often unballasted or in a bed of cinders; tracks serving fuel depots generally had a dirty, grimy, oily appearance. This was especially true in the era before environmental safety protocols were in place. Through the 1960s, the area around the tracks near the tank car connectors was subject to thousands of small-scale spills and drips over decades of use (a pint here, a couple of gallons there), giving the whole area a grungy look.

Some farmer's cooperatives sold fuel along with feed and other products, including Farmer's Equity in Wolf Point, Mont., in 1941. The horizontal tanks are atop steel girder racks. The truck at right has a pair of crosswise tanks mounted on a flatbed chassis. *Marion Post Wolcott, Library of Congress*

Modern facilities—any since the founding of the Environmental Protection Agency in 1970—are required to have spill containment, with permanent or temporary pans under the tank car connections and anywhere that pipes or connections might leak. Another modern touch is safety railings on unloading racks, with platforms that extend to the car tops.

Along the track, there will be a derail between the dealer and the main line, with a lock on the mainline switch. These ensure that a car accidentally rolling away doesn't foul

Horizontal tanks at dealers were often mounted on concrete pedestals, as the two tanks at left. The later tank at far right is on a steel frame pedestal. *Marion Post Wolcott, Library of Congress*

A delivery truck is being filled at a two-sided loading rack at a dealer in Bordentown, N.J., in 1974, as two other trucks are parked and waiting. *Jeff Wilson collection*

the main line. And don't forget signs indicating limited clearance near the racks, unloading platforms, or other obstructions.

The pump was contained in a pumphouse, generally a small windowless building adjacent to the storage tanks. Piping to the tracks could be above ground or buried; pipes to tanks could be above ground.

Although uncommon, there were locations where early bulk oil dealers were located away from the tracks, but were still rail-served. At these depots, pipes ran underground from loading racks to the storage tanks and depot, which could be a block or two (or even farther) away.

Warehouse and ancillary buildings

Warehouses and other buildings varied in construction style and size based on the amount of business and types of products handled by the jobber. Some were wood frame buildings, but corrugated-metal-sheathed structures were common, and some were concrete block. A loading dock (usually concrete) with large doors faced away from the tracks for truck loading; the office was often on this side, with a smaller door and a window or two marking its location. The warehouse may or may not abut the tracks; space was often tight at dealers, so the warehouse might be separate. If it is next to the tracks, a loading platform will be located on that side, as well.

Warehouses hold products such as cases of motor oil (for delivery to service stations) and 55-gallon drums of lube oil, solvents, greases, and other products. Depots may receive these products via rail, but some did not sell enough to warrant delivery of a full railcar. Another common delivery method for these was by less-than-carload (LCL) shipment—the jobber would send a truck to the local train station to pick up the products upon arrival. Delivery by truck became more common by the 1960s.

If the warehouse was not adjacent to the tracks, the jobber would move products by hand. Another option was to back up a van truck or stake truck to the boxcar, load products aboard, and transfer them to the warehouse.

The warehouse could also hold other needed tools and parts. Many jobbers installed and serviced gas pumps, home furnaces and heaters, and other appliances, as well.

Truck loading

The primary business of a fuel depot was delivery of bulk fuel products, so the truck loading facility was prominent. Small jobbers usually had a single rack, but some larger dealers had a longer rack to allow loading two or more trucks at once.

Loading racks were tall, mounted on platforms to allow easy access to the truck tank rooftop hatches. Racks were usually located adjacent to (and sometimes as a part of) the pumphouse. Multiple standpipes (one for each product handled), each color-coded, allow loading through the top

Many smaller LPG dealers were served by rail into the 2000s. This Ferrellgas dealer in Litchfield, Minn., received one or two cars of LPG on its spur (behind the tanks at right) into the 2010s. *Jeff Wilson*

A Procor tank car is parked at the unloading rack at the Litchfield LPG dealer. The rack has a drop-down access walkway to the tank car platform. The eduction and vent connections are all flexible hoses. *Jeff Wilson*

hatch above each compartment. Trucks have up to six compartments to handle separate products. The loading pipes look much like gas-pump nozzles with squeeze handles, but bigger. Meters on the pipe stands record the amount of fuel pumped.

Fuel depots used a variety of trucks to deliver products (Chapter 8 shows several photos and provides details on these vehicles). A small jobber may have a single small straight truck or two; larger dealers will have a variety of vehicles, including small straight trucks and tractor-trailers for bulk deliveries, and vans, enclosed trucks, step vans, or pickup trucks to deliver non-bulk goods and to provide service and repair calls.

These vehicles may simply be parked outside at the depot (a great way to show off your scale vehicle collection) or they may be in a larger garage or shed (a more common practice in areas that see heavy snowfall and bad weather).

Trucks of branded jobbers typically carry paint schemes and logos of the brand itself, with the local owner lettered on the door or side of the tank.

The Litchfield LPG dealer has horizontal storage tanks of 30,000- and 18,000-gallon capacities. The truck loading connections are at the end of the tank. Smaller propane tanks, including tall 100-gallon "bottles," are on the platform next to the control shack. *Jeff Wilson*

Locations, signs, details

Larger towns and small cities often had multiple dealers in close proximity to each other, often located on the same or adjoining rail spurs. As noted earlier, this was because fuel depots were often on railroad-owned property. This made it handy for the railroad to have dealers at one location, simplifying switching and train operations.

A town served by two or more railroads might have a group of two or three jobbers located in one part of town on one railroad, with another two or three jobbers located across town on the other rail line.

The drawback of this arrangement was that as soon as a dealer dropped its rail service, it usually had to quickly find another location for its operation, as the railroad had no interest in leasing property to a business they no longer served. This is why many small dealers vanished from railside soon after ceasing rail operations.

Branding was very important in the oil industry, and dealers tied to specific brands generally had logos of their parent company in prominent locations on tanks and buildings. Spelling out the company name across a row of tanks was another common practice. There would usually be a sign with the company's official name—"Medford Oil Co.," for example—along with the parent company logos.

Other details around the depot included 55-gallon drums, which were sometimes stored outside. They could be stacked or placed horizontally on barrel racks (drum racks): pairs of metal tracks at a slight angle, allowing drums to rest by gravity at one end, but be easily rolled to the other (see the Texaco dealer photo on page 43).

Other outdoor details included portable tanks, such as those destined for farms or businesses, or fuel-oil tanks destined for residential use; old signs, new signs, gas pumps and parts, fork trucks, and dollies and hand carts.

Operations

The specific customers of a jobber varied by location. The company that owned the oil depot often also owned one or more service stations, giving it built-in customers to serve. The jobber could also contract with other non-owned service stations to provide fuel and other products.

Fuel dealers in small towns and rural areas served farms, which usually had small on-site fuel storage (tanks ranging from 100 to 500 gallons) for gasoline or diesel fuel. As coal gave way to fuel oil for heating in the 1920s and later, fuel dealers delivered to homes in both towns and rural areas. A typical in-home fuel oil tank held 275 gallons. (Homes in large cities were generally served by gas pipelines, with coal gas giving way to natural gas by the mid-1900s.)

Another major customer group for jobbers is contract customers. These are larger users who buy in large enough quantities to receive a discount from retail price. They include construction companies, fleet trucking companies, bus companies, airports, marinas, larger industries, and public utilities.

Railroad operations are straightforward, with a local freight dropping off a car or cars as needed and picking up empties. These operations could be daily at larger dealers; smaller dealers will see a car every few days, with multi-compartment tanks more common. Along with tank cars, which make up the bulk of traffic, don't forget a boxcar every few weeks to deliver packaged products like lube oil and grease in cases and drums.

Keep in mind that since revenue-service tank cars are all privately owned, a branded dealer would only receive tank cars leased or owned by the parent company. In other words, a Sinclair jobber wouldn't receive cars lettered for (and controlled by) Deep Rock or Texaco. A boxcar of oil drums being delivered, however, could wear the markings of any railroad.

Bulk dealers had to be very aware of the rate of products going out compared to storage space when placing an order with their suppliers, especially since it could take three or more days for a tank car to arrive. Transit time varied by individual refinery, the distance involved, and the level of rail traffic on the lines the tank car would travel.

Ensuring adequate space to store an inbound load was vital, but making a mistake the other way—running out of a product—could cost not only sales, but also customers.

Shift to trucks

By the 1960s, the trend was moving toward larger and fewer dealers, as well as toward tractor-trailer delivery to most dealers that remained. Trucks were becoming larger, and the growing interstate highway system drastically cut transport times for trucks, making it possible to extend delivery territories.

Product pipeline networks had continued expanding, and oil companies were building tank terminals at regular intervals along pipelines at distances that ensured complete coverage for their territories by truck. Truck delivery was faster, cutting the cushion between order and delivery time, allowing dealers to more precisely manage inventory. The decision to switch to trucks was often that of the distributing company, not the individual fuel dealer.

Even though most fuel dealers are no longer served by rail, a few still remain—mainly high-volume dealers at the fringes of truck routes, making rail transport still a viable option.

LPG dealers

Liquified petroleum gas (LPG, a mix of propane and butane that's adjusted depending upon season, weather, and intended use) became popular as a home heating fuel beginning in the 1930s. It was marketed as an alternative to fuel oil, replacing coal for furnaces for rural and small-town

A driver poses for a photo while his truck is being filled at the Saf-T-Gas LPG terminal at Plant City, Fla., in 1970. You can see the hose connections at the rear of the truck and the chock placed behind the far rear wheel during loading. *Jeff Wilson collection*

A worker connects the unloading hoses to a new whalebelly-style LP car at a Philgas distributor in the early 1960s. A pair of tractor-trailer transports in the background will be loaded to make deliveries. *Trains Magazine collection*

homes that didn't have access to natural gas lines, and is still widely used in those areas.

Liquefied petroleum gas compresses easily to a liquid, so it's reasonably easy to transport by tank car and truck. But it doesn't travel well by pipeline, so it remains more dependent upon rail transport than natural gas and home-heating oil. Many LPG dealers still receive deliveries by rail, especially in northern climates where winter is severe.

Phillips Petroleum began the push to LPG in the late 1920s, marketing its product as Philgas, and worked to set up distributors. Skelly (Skelgas), Pure (Puregas), and others soon followed. Although the Depression slowed this trend, by the 1940s and '50s, LPG dealers could be found across the country. Some dealers handling gasoline added LPG to their business lines, but more common were separate dealers specializing in propane and butane.

These dealers were often tied to home-appliance and furnace dealers selling products branded with the LPG company name—you could, for example, purchase a Skelgas kitchen range with very attractive financing in the 1950s, and the nice Skelgas dealer would set up your propane tanks and make sure you had prompt fuel delivery whenever needed.

The basic appearance and operations of an LPG jobber are quite similar to the bulk fuel dealers described earlier, but with some significant differences in storage and how the product is handled.

The storage tanks are pressure vessels, rated at 500 psi or more (LPG pressure varies depending upon its temperature, but is generally liquified at just over 100 psi). Tanks are horizontal with hemispherical ends, and are welded; you won't see riveted seams or flat tank ends on an LPG tank. They rest on saddles above ground.

Size varies by the amount of business done by the dealer, but individual tanks are typically 15,000 to 30,000 gallons, and a dealer may have two or more tanks. The more modern the facility, the larger it tends to be.

Tank car unloading is done at the top of the car, so a trackside rack is provided with steps and platform. Typically, a fold-down ramp provides access to the car's top bonnet. Three hoses are used: two product eduction lines, plus a compressed-air line that keeps the car's interior at the proper pressure to ensure that the product remains liquid. The lines are connected and the valves opened to allow the product to flow.

A neighboring building with valves and equipment control piping routes

A train is spotting a tank car at Koppy's Propane, a medium-sized LPG distributor at Good Spring, Pa., in 2017. Note the concrete barriers between the drive path and the storage tanks at right. *Scott A. Hartley*

the product to the correct tanks. This building may also house equipment for filling small LPG tanks, as well as loading bulk delivery trucks.

Other details at an LPG dealer, besides trucks and vehicles, include empty 500- and 1,000-gallon tanks (ready for delivery and installation or being serviced), and 100-gallon bottles and smaller tanks waiting to be filled. LPG dealers are more likely than gas/fuel oil dealers to have security fences and gating around the complex.

Operations

A small-town dealer might have multiple bulk trucks to deliver to tanks at homes in towns and in the country. Most homes with high-volume use have large, permanent tanks outdoors. The familiar hot-dog-shaped, horizontal tank holds 500 gallons; larger versions hold up to 1,000 gallons.

LPG is also commonly handled in various smaller containers. The familiar 20-pound (five gallon) tank is small and squatty; it's typically used for barbecue grills and portable camping trailers. Consumers can get these today at a hardware or home-improvement store, as well as LPG dealers. An LPG dealer typically services these retail outlets, picking up empty containers, filling them at the plant, and dropping off loaded ones.

Common for small-volume home use, especially in warmer climes, are tall, vertical 100-gallon tanks with top-mounted fittings, nicknamed "bottles." They are portable, and when empty, the consumer can either bring it to the LP dealer to exchange for a full one, or the dealer will bring a new one to the consumer and exchange it.

To deliver and service bottles, most dealers have vans or stake-bed trucks, with bottles secured to the truck body. Most dealers also have trucks to provide service and repairs, and as with fuel-oil dealers, many LPG dealers (especially through the 1960s) provided installation and service on gas furnaces and appliances.

Rail service and frequency of course depends on the amount of business. Remember that railcars carrying LPG will be high-pressure cars in dedicated service, so standard general-purpose non-pressure cars shouldn't be spotted at an LPG dealer. See Chapter 6 for details on pressure tank cars.

Many LPG wholesalers and dealers still receive shipments by rail, but the trend is toward larger distributors that can receive multiple tank car shipments at once. Small-town dealers that get a carload at a time can still be found, but are becoming rare. The small dealers that remain are often supplied by semi-truck from larger distributors.

CHAPTER FOUR

Pipeline terminals and tank farms

The tank terminal of Colonial Oil Industries in Savannah, Ga., in 2017 features tanks of many sizes, two parallel tracks with a loading/unloading platform between them, and multiple truck loading stations. The facility also receives shipments by water via the Savannah River, which is just out of sight to the right. The company distributes fuel to gas stations of several brands plus unbranded stations. *Carol M. Highsmith, Library of Congress*

Methods for distribution of finished petroleum products changed radically in the decade following World War II. The product pipelines that rapidly expanded throughout the country served and terminated at numerous large distribution terminals, which took much long-distance refinery-to-bulk-dealer traffic from railroads.

A new pipeline terminal is under construction in Spokane, Wash., in 1959, with a rail spur at upper left. The four tanks at right all have floating roofs. The earth berms are all the same height, so larger tanks require larger areas surrounded by the berms. *Jeff Wilson collection*

These pipeline terminals, often known as "tank farms," then ship products via truck, rail, and sometimes ship to smaller local dealers or directly to larger customers. Terminals feature multiple large storage tanks that are much larger than those at local dealers or jobbers (see Chapter 3), with individual capacities of 100,000 barrels and more.

From the 1930s through the 1950s, railroads still played a significant role in moving products from tank terminals to local dealers, with hauls of a few hundred miles common—longer where pipelines hadn't yet reached a region. However, by the 1960s the growth of interstate highways, increasing truck size, and further pipeline and terminal expansion led to trucks taking most of this traffic from rails. By the 1970s, the vast majority of this traffic was by truck, and although some are still served by rail, this is now quite limited.

We'll start with a look at pipelines. Even though they're largely hidden and not subject to modeling, understanding their history and how they work will enable modeling tank farms, refineries, dealers, and associated railroad operations more realistically. We'll follow by examining details of tank farms and terminals and see how railroad operations at these facilities evolved over time.

Pipeline history

Today, most petroleum products are shipped via a vast network of pipelines that crisscross the country. The U.S. currently has about 230,000 miles of crude oil and liquid product pipelines, plus more than 1.4 million miles of natural gas pipelines.

The modern pipeline can trace its roots back several thousand years, to bamboo pipes and stone aqueducts, but the first truly modern installations date to 1807 in London, when a network of iron pipes was first used to carry coal gas for lighting. Their use soon spread throughout Britain, and several U.S. cities had gas pipelines by the 1830s. By 1860, there were nearly 300 coal gas plants in U.S. cities, serving 4.8 million customers. Since it was distributed by gas mains, it was broadly known as "mains gas."

The establishment of the first oil well in 1859 in Titusville, Pa., (Chapter 1) soon led to small pipelines for moving crude oil from wells to refineries. These started as small operations over short distances of a few miles or less. The efficiencies of this were significant, as the pipeline replaced the need for multiple teams of horses pulling wagons or railcars for short hauls.

The "Big Inch" is a 24"-diameter pipeline that was built in 1943-1944 to connect refineries and oilfields of the Southwest to Eastern ports. This section has just been given a coat of hot asphalt paint prior to lowering it into its trench. Pipelines eliminated much long-distance petroleum traffic for railroads. *Library of Congress*

While refining became more specialized and refineries grew in size and number, new oil deposits were also discovered, increasing the distance from wells to refineries. By 1900, there were about 6,800 miles of crude pipelines operating in the country, including a cross-country line from Texas and Oklahoma oil fields to East Coast refineries. The first finished-product (gasoline) pipeline in the U.S. began operating in Wyoming in 1918, a 3" pipe carrying gasoline 40 miles from Salt Creek to Casper.

Pipe-fabrication technology was improving, moving from small-diameter (2"-4") wrought-iron, then cast-iron pipe to large-diameter (14" and larger) seamless steel pipe with welded joints. The larger pipes substantially increased capacity and were safer than iron pipes.

Magnolia Petroleum gets credit for the first major broad-diameter pipe installation, a 217-mile-long, all-welded 14-18" pipeline from northern Louisiana to Beaumont, Texas in 1925.

By the late 1920s, natural gas was beginning to replace manufactured (coal) gas in U.S. cities, carried by long-distance pipelines from oil fields in the Southwest to the Midwest and East. By the early 1930s, natural gas accounted for 80 percent of the market, compared to 20 percent for coal gas. Even though natural gas was not carried by rail, this move affected other types of rail transport. Manufactured gas plants, which railroads supplied with coal and carried off the byproducts of coke and ammonia, became rare by the early 1950s.

World War II and later

Gasoline supplies were in a critical state as World War II loomed and the U.S. entered the war. There was a sudden increased demand for fuel to East Coast ports, but tanker ships —the favored transport—were being torpedoed off the coast, cutting crude oil and gasoline shipments from the Gulf and Southwest to refineries and ports in the East. Railroads were scrambling to make up the losses with solid trains of petroleum (see Chapter 7 for details), but more capacity and production were needed.

To provide this capacity, the government funded construction of a pair of major pipeline projects that would come to be known as the "Big Inch" and "Little Inch" (together the "Inch Pipelines").

The Big Inch was a 24" crude-oil pipeline running about 1,200 miles from Longview, Texas, northeast to Norris City, Ill., and Phoenixville, Pa., and then in two branches to Linden, N.J., and Philadelphia (Chester Junction, Pa.). It supplied oil to Midwestern and Eastern refineries.

The Little Inch (or "Little Big Inch") was a 1,400-mile, 20" pipeline

Tanks are often painted with their owners' logos or brand names. This is an Atlantic Refining tank farm in the Southwest during World War II. These scenes lend themselves to modeling as photos on backdrops. *Library of Congress*

for refined products. It originated at Beaumont, Texas, then ran to Little Rock, Ark.; from there it shared the right-of-way of the Big Inch to the Midwest and East.

Construction began on the Big Inch in June 1942 and the Little Inch in January 1943; the first crude delivery was in August 1943 and product in March 1944. At capacity, the Big Inch carried 334,456 barrels of crude per day, and the Little Inch 239,844 barrels of gasoline per day.

Following the war, the pipelines were sold to private owners, and both were converted to natural gas. In 1957 the Little Inch was converted back to liquid petroleum use.

As an aside, railroads were largely responsible for delivering the pipe for the construction of the lines, a staggering project that required more than 21,100 gondola loads of the material.

Pipeline construction continued over the next decades, with 57,000 miles of product pipelines and 148,000 miles of crude pipelines by 1964 and about 230,000 miles of pipelines today. They are centered in the primary oilfield and refining regions in the Southwest. Cushing, Okla., which has

Storage tank sizes and capacities

Dia. (ft.)	Ht. (ft.)	Barrels	Gallons
22	24	1,620	68,200
25	24	2,090	88,100
35	24	4,110	172,700
40	24	5,370	225,600
51	24	8,730	366,700
60	24	12,000	507,600
85	24	24,200	1,018,700
22	32	2,160	90,900
25	32	2,790	117,500
35	32	5,480	230,300
40	32	7,160	300,800
51	32	11,600	489,000
60	32	16,100	676,000
85	32	32,300	1,358,300
100	32	44,700	1,880,000
52	40	15,100	635,400
60	40	20,100	846,000
80	40	35,800	1,504,000
100	40	55,900	2,350,000
120	40	80,500	3,384,000

To calculate the volume of a round tank, use this formula (using measurements in inches):

$\pi r^2 \times$ height $\times$ .004329 = tank capacity in gallons

("r" is the radius of the tank; radius and height are both in inches)

Tank farms at ports, such as this one near Houston, Texas, in 2011, can ship and receive oil by water. Note the rail storage yards as well as the tracks for tank car loading and unloading. *Carol M. Highsmith, Library of Congress*

This tank farm has access roads (with streetlights) atop the berms among the tanks. Steps allow access; control valves and piping are located around each tank. *Mike Small*

A Southern Ry. steam locomotive prepares to switch a cut of tank cars into the Standard Oil Co. pipeline terminal at Friendship, N.C., in 1944. The crew is waiting for security personnel to open the gates at the chain-link fence. Note the fire hydrant in the foreground at left. *Standard Oil Co.*

had many refineries over the years, is currently the self-proclaimed "pipeline crossroads of the world." It is indeed that for crude oil, with more than 90 million barrels of capacity at tank farms with connections to dozens of pipelines heading in all directions.

By the 2020s, railroads carried only about 3% of total petroleum traffic. Pipelines carry about 70%, with 23% by water and 4% by truck.

Pipeline operations

Pipelines carrying liquids are either common carriers or privately owned by a single company. Common-carrier pipelines, like a common-carrier railroad or trucking company, are available to multiple shippers wishing to use them at standard published rates (once subject to Interstate Commerce Commission approval).

A pipeline starts at a refinery, port, oilfield, or other terminal. Multiple products can be sent in the same pipeline. One method to separate them is with a "pig," a small, flexible plug that travels through the pipeline between shipments (pigs are also used to clean the pipe interior). Products can also sometimes be shipped without pigs.

Pumping stations are located periodically along each pipeline to keep product flowing. The distance between pumping stations varies by terrain (and grades) and size of the pipeline. Other installations include stations with valves and sensors that monitor flow and that can shut down and isolate sections of line.

A pipeline may serve a single terminal or refinery, or it can serve several terminals along its length. It was the goal of most major oil companies by the 1970s to have tank terminals located throughout their operating regions spaced to allow economical delivery by truck.

Tank terminals

A pipeline terminal or tank farm, although large, can be a very modelable subject on a layout. These terminals, where products are received via pipeline from refineries and ports (or directly by ship if located at a port or waterway) and stored on a large scale, began appearing as product pipelines began expanding from the 1930s onward. Through the 1960s, most were served by rail. As tank farms have increased in size and highway transport has also grown, trucks have taken more business from rails in transporting finished products.

The layout of a tank farm is pretty straightforward. They're much simpler than a refinery (Chapter 2), but significantly larger than a bulk fuel distributor (Chapter 3). A tank terminal can take up several acres of space, most of which is occupied by large storage tanks of various sizes

A foreman checks cars being switched into the Standard tank terminal in Friendship, N.C., in 1944, as brakemen ride on the rear tank car and atop the boxcar to pass signals to the engine crew. *Standard Oil Co.*

and designs. A large pumphouse or pumping station will be included, with prominent piping leading to tanks and other structures.

Depending upon the pipeline, a terminal could be exclusive to one oil company (like the Champlin terminal on page 65), or it could serve multiple companies (such as the Colonial terminal on page 54).

The rail siding is usually at one edge of the terminal, with a long elevated platform along the track or tracks. The extent of the rail spur depends on the size of the terminal and the percentage of products the terminal ships by rail. Larger terminals may have multiple tracks (one on each side of the loading platform) or an additional pair of tracks with its own center platform, usually all parallel to each other. Another track or two may enter the terminal for bringing in other products, construction equipment, or parts.

Tank car loading racks at pipeline terminals follow the same designs as those at refineries. Several cars are being loaded at a Standard facility in Baton Rouge, La., in 1943. Note the grimy, oily appearance of the track and surrounding ground. *Standard Oil Co.*

Some terminals also handle non-bulk products (packaged or barrels). These will reside in a warehouse building with a truck dock, and possibly a rail siding, as well.

Truck loading racks mirror those at refineries and are designed to allow multiple trucks to load at once.

Security is a priority at these facilities, just as at refineries, so they will be surrounded by chain-link fences topped by barbed wire or razor wire. The rail entrance will have gates that

Workers prepare to unload oil from a set of General American TankTrain cars, which are interconnected with hoses. This allows multiple cars to be loaded or unloaded from one connection point. The terminal is at Essexville, Mich., on Grand Trunk Western in 1978. *George Drury*

Since the 1970s, tank car loading and unloading areas will have permanent or portable catch pans underneath cars to limit effects of spills. *Jeff Wilson*

are locked when closed; simulating the unlocking of these gates before switching the complex can add to operational interest. The truck/vehicle entrance will also have a gate and a guard shack or building, with all inbound vehicles checking in. Vehicle paths will go throughout the terminal to allow guards and workers to do rounds, including around the perimeter and through the tank areas (sometimes on the berms, as the photo on page 58 shows).

Operation is straightforward. The pipeline delivers fuel and oil products, which are routed to the appropriate storage tanks by controls in the pumping/control building. Transport trucks (mainly tractor-trailers) are continually arriving, with most terminals operating 24 hours a day.

Rail spurs are handled by local freights or dedicated switch jobs that drop off empty tank cars and pick up loaded ones. Trains can also deliver loads of ethanol and other gasoline additives to be added to gasoline when trucks are loaded for final delivery (a process called "splash blending"). These can also arrive by truck.

As an example, the Colonial terminal on page 54 delivers fuel to gas stations of eight different brands. Each brand has its proprietary additives that must be stored on site (the numerous small storage tanks near the truck loading platforms on page 54) and added to trucks delivering a specific branded product.

Tank details

Tanks are built in a tremendous variety of styles and sizes, with a wide range of diameters and heights. The largest tanks at refineries and tank farms can hold a million gallons or more. The chart on page 57 shows some examples of the capacities of tanks based on their measurements (height and diameter).

Riveted steel construction was common through the 1930s, with welded tanks becoming more common by the 1940s and later. Tanks holding liquids are round; roofs can be solid or floating. Solid-roof tanks have roofs that are either elliptical (rounded edges that flatten toward the top) or have a slight conical shape, with the peak in the middle. Both shapes are designed to deflect rainwater.

Floating-roof tanks, which began appearing in the 1920s, are designed to eliminate empty space above volatile liquids, limiting loss from evaporation and lowering the buildup of explosive

Four trucks can be loaded at once at the two-sided covered loading rack at this 1940s-era Gulf terminal. *Gulf Oil photo by Arthur Thomas Spohn; Mont Switzer collection*

vapors. These roofs are steel disks with built-in floats on the underside (similar to boat pontoons), allowing the roof to rest directly on the product itself. The roof rises and falls with the fluid level of the product in the tank. A flexible seal running around the rim of the roof keeps vapor or liquid from escaping.

Floating roofs can be external (external floating roof tank, EFRT) or internal (IFRT). EFRT roofs have a very distinctive appearance when viewed from above, as the tank level is readily apparent. A view of a tank farm or refinery will often show tanks with roofs at varying heights. On an IFRT, there's an external fixed roof, with the floating roof inside the tank structure. This is done to keep rain and snow from collecting on the floating roof. From the outside, these are hard to tell from a solid-roof tank.

Pipes connect the tank to the pumping station, with inlet and outlet pipes at the base of the tank.

Each tank has an access ladder or stairs to its roof. On small tanks, this can be a ladder with safety cage, but most larger tanks have steps that either spiral upward around the tank itself or stairs that angle upward in a straight line from a distant anchor point. On the roof will be a manway and vents. Modern tanks have built-in fire containment systems with piping to the top that can direct foam directly below onto the tank contents. Other features include float gauges and monitoring equipment that can detect fire or abnormal heat or pressure.

Tanks containing hazardous liquids have containment dikes surrounding them to limit the environmental effects if a leak occurs. At tank farms, this usually means a heavy earth berm or dam between tanks. Most piping is underground, but as photos show, pipes with valves and control equipment protrude from the ground around the tanks.

Tanks are typically painted silver or white to deflect sunlight and heat. Large corporate logos and lettering on tanks were common into the 1960s, but are not as common at modern plants. Numbers and warning signs ("inflammable" and "no smoking") are also common.

Tanks holding pressurized gases (propane, butane, LPG) are welded steel pressure vessels, distinct from tanks carrying liquids at normal atmospheric pressure. They are built in two basic configurations: spherical or longitudinal with hemispherical (rounded) or elliptical ends. Refineries are more likely to have large, spherical tanks, which are stronger but more expensive to build. Spherical tanks were named "Hortonspheres" for their designer, Horace E. Horton of Chicago Bridge & Iron Co.; the first was built in 1923.

Most non-spherical LPG tanks are mounted horizontally, although some early installations had groups of these tanks mounted vertically.

MODELING TIPS

Even though tank terminals are huge facilities, their design makes them quite modelable. Because the rail sidings are generally at one edge, you can plausibly model the spurs and loading rack in a fairly narrow space, with most (or all) of the tanks as photo-print backdrops. You can also model a tank or two in the foreground if you have room, or in a corner.

See the modeling tips section in Chapter 2 for ideas on storage tanks, as well as the chapters on tank cars (Chapters 5 and 6) and trucks (Chapter 8).

This tank terminal in North Carolina has a covered drive-through loading structure with four parallel bays. One of the facility's storage tanks (and part of a tall berm) is visible at left. *Mike Small*

Case Study: Champlin Refining Co.

Champlin's only refinery was located in the company's home city of Enid, Okla. It was expanded multiple times, eventually to a 24,000 barrel/day capacity in 1948. *Oklahoma Historical Society*

Dozens of oil companies served the country in the steam and early diesel eras. Although the market was dominated by several national brands (Gulf, Shell, and Texaco, for example), many regional companies were successful in selling to smaller areas, from a single state to a dozen or more.

Understanding how these companies integrated operations can help us better understand how railroads played a role in their product marketing and distribution. These companies varied in how they did business: buying crude from various sources and either producing products at their own refineries or contracting with independent refineries.

One such regional was Champlin Refining Co., based in Enid, Okla. The company began operations in the 1910s and grew to become the largest fully integrated, privately owned oil company in the country. "Fully integrated" means the company had its own wells, refinery, distributors, and service stations/dealers.

The company's founder, H.H. Champlin, got his start by taking out an oilfield lease in 1916 and drilling several successful wells. His wells were soon producing enough crude that he was having difficulty profitably selling it all, so in 1917 he purchased a small (200 bbl/day) refinery in Enid and began Champlin Refining Co. The refinery had expanded to 16,000 bbl/day by 1921.

Champlin made the decision early to keep the company fully integrated. With that in mind, in 1920 the company began producing packaged lubricating oil at its refinery. This allowed Champlin to sell a full range of products through independent jobbers and distributors. The company's first branded filling station opened in Enid in 1923, and by the mid-1920s, Champlin was selling its products in a six-state area centering on Oklahoma. Distribution was by rail and truck. Inbound crude arrived by pipeline, with 500 miles of pipeline running from Enid to multiple oil fields. Champlin also traded crude with other oil companies.

Champlin had a significant fleet of tank cars into the 1960s, most of which wore this white-and-black scheme with the company name and logo. Number 580 is an 8,000-gallon ARA III car built by Pennsylvania Tank Car Co. in 1923. *Ted Culotta collection*

The company expanded its reach in the late 1930s by building a product pipeline northward from Enid. It was among the first private product pipelines in the country, used for both gasoline and fuel oil. The line eventually hosted three tank farm/distribution terminals. From the refinery the line first traveled to Hutchinson, Kan., then to Superior, Neb., and finally Rock Rapids, Iowa, 516 miles from Enid. The pipeline was completed in 1940 and had a capacity of 9,800 bbl/day.

By the 1940s, Champlin had wholesalers and service stations in 20 states from Oklahoma and New Mexico to the Dakotas, Minnesota, and Wisconsin. In 1948 the refinery was expanded to 24,000 bbl/day capacity. The company had 800 branded service stations by the late 1970s, with the heaviest concentration around Oklahoma.

Champlin's tank terminals, like the refinery itself, shipped products via tank car and truck to jobbers throughout Champlin's operating territory. A private phone line and teletype system was used to communicate and place orders among the terminals and refinery offices.

This aerial view from 1956 shows the Champlin pipeline terminal at Rock Rapids, Iowa. It's a compact facility with six large tanks and several small ones; the truck loadout is on the circular drive at upper right. It was served by a Rock Island branch; seven tank cars rest on the loading rack spur at right, while another two are on the spur to the warehouse. *Historic Aerials (historicaerials.com)*

Champlin had a significant fleet of tank cars (reporting marks HHCX), mainly older 8,000-gallon ARA III cars for carrying gasoline and oil. The company had 712 cars in 1943. In 1955, 651 cars were still operating, and in 1962, there were 558. After that, numbers dropped significantly, to 248 in 1968 and 72 in 1971.

As an example, the Rock Rapids terminal (above) mainly served the company's Sioux Falls region, which included the Dakotas, Minnesota, Wisconsin, and northern Iowa. In the late 1940s, that terminal was shipping 225,000 gallons of products or more daily by truck, plus up to eight tank cars. The tank cars served the most distant jobbers in the region.

Whether a dealer received fuel by truck or tank car was largely up to the jobbers, who paid the freight charges to have products delivered from the tank terminals. They could use their own or hired trucks or use Champlin tank cars. Each of the terminals sold gasoline, kerosene, diesel fuel, and lube oil (including packaged oil). Additives were blended into products at the terminals.

Rail service at the pipeline terminals continued into the late 1960s, but shifted to truck-only after that point. Most refining companies did this by the 1970s, so most jobbers—regardless of brand—lost the option of receiving products by rail, except for special situations involving long distances and high volume.

Champlin remained independent until 1953, when it went public. It was purchased by The Chicago Corp. in 1955, but continued operating as Champlin into the early 1980s, when the refinery closed, the pipeline was sold, the brand was discontinued, and operations were sold to other companies.

Relative size

To provide a size comparison to Champlin, look at a national company, Sinclair (Consolidated Oil Corp.). In the 1930s, Sinclair was the country's eighth-largest oil company, with five refineries and 14,000 miles of pipelines. Sinclair had 6,000 tank cars serving 2,100 bulk depots and 8,100 service stations.

A transport semi rolls out of a Champlin tank terminal in the 1960s. The company's slogan at the time was "A great name in the Great Plains." *Jeff Wilson collection*

A Champlin delivery driver and his dog pose with his truck in 1940. The truck has a sign promoting the company's HI-V-I motor oil. *Jeff Wilson collection*

CHAPTER FIVE

Gasoline, crude, and fuel oil tank cars

The expansion-dome-equipped, non-insulated general-purpose tank car was the backbone of the petroleum fleet from the steam era into the 1960s. This 8,000-gallon Gulf car was built by Standard Steel Car in 1920 and is in its final months of service at a gasoline terminal in 1960. Many oil companies proudly put their logos on their cars through this era. *John Ingles; J. David Ingles collection*

Railroads have carried petroleum products since the oil industry's beginnings. The first tank cars were wooden, but tank cars were among the first iron and steel freight cars starting in the 1870s. Cars have evolved significantly in construction methods and size since then, as railroads continue to carry crude oil and refined products.

Common liquid petroleum products that have been transported by tank car include crude oil itself, along with gasoline, kerosene, motor oil, lubricating oil, diesel fuel, and various grades of fuel oil, along with residuals such as asphalt. Doing this has long been the job of the general-purpose tank car, officially known as a non-pressure tank car. By ARA and AAR classifications, tank cars are type "T," with TM meaning a general-service tank car and TMI a general-service insulated tank car.

Liquified gases, such as propane and butane (known commonly as liquified petroleum gas, or LPG), are carried in high-pressure tank cars as described in Chapter 6.

Let's start with a look at early general-purpose cars, then see how they've evolved. We'll examine why tank cars are privately owned and review the major owners and leasing companies.

Early design and evolution

When the first crude oil wells began producing in the early 1860s, oil was typically transported from wells to refineries in barrels loaded atop flatcars or in gondolas, which was cumbersome. The first true tank car appeared in 1865. The Densmore car (named after the brothers who developed it), an example of which is seen below, featured a converted flatcar with a pair of vertical wooden tanks with pine staves and strap-iron bands. These tanks were slightly conical, as they tapered in 6" at the top. Each tank stood 6 feet tall and held roughly 40 barrels of oil.

The tank tops were flat with a hatch for loading; unloading was through a pipe and valve at the bottom of the tank side. The first converted flatcars were 27 feet long; later cars were built for the purpose and shortened to 21'-3", eliminating the wide gap between tanks. Some later cars had three tanks or horizontal wood tanks.

The transport distances involved at the time were generally short, but the wood construction of thsee cars made them still not an ideal solution. They often leaked, and they were not long-lasting. Railroads, however, did not want to invest in the then-considerable expense of building cast-iron or steel cars, especially since they were good for only a single commodity, and then only for only a one-way trip. Railroads were also unsure about what the future would bring for the oil industry and whether the business was a boom that would soon go bust. The result was that tank cars would be built and operated by private owners and leasing companies instead of railroads (see the section on car ownership on page 78).

In 1867, the first cars featuring a horizontal iron tank appeared. The tanks were mounted on wooden flat cars. The first tank car with its own frame was built by Empire Transportation Company in 1869. Cars

The first tank cars of the 1860s had pairs of vertical wooden tanks atop a flatcar deck. Each tank held about 40 barrels of oil. The tanks were not long lasting and were prone to leaks. This car had archbar trucks and link-and-pin couplers.
Union Tank Car Co.

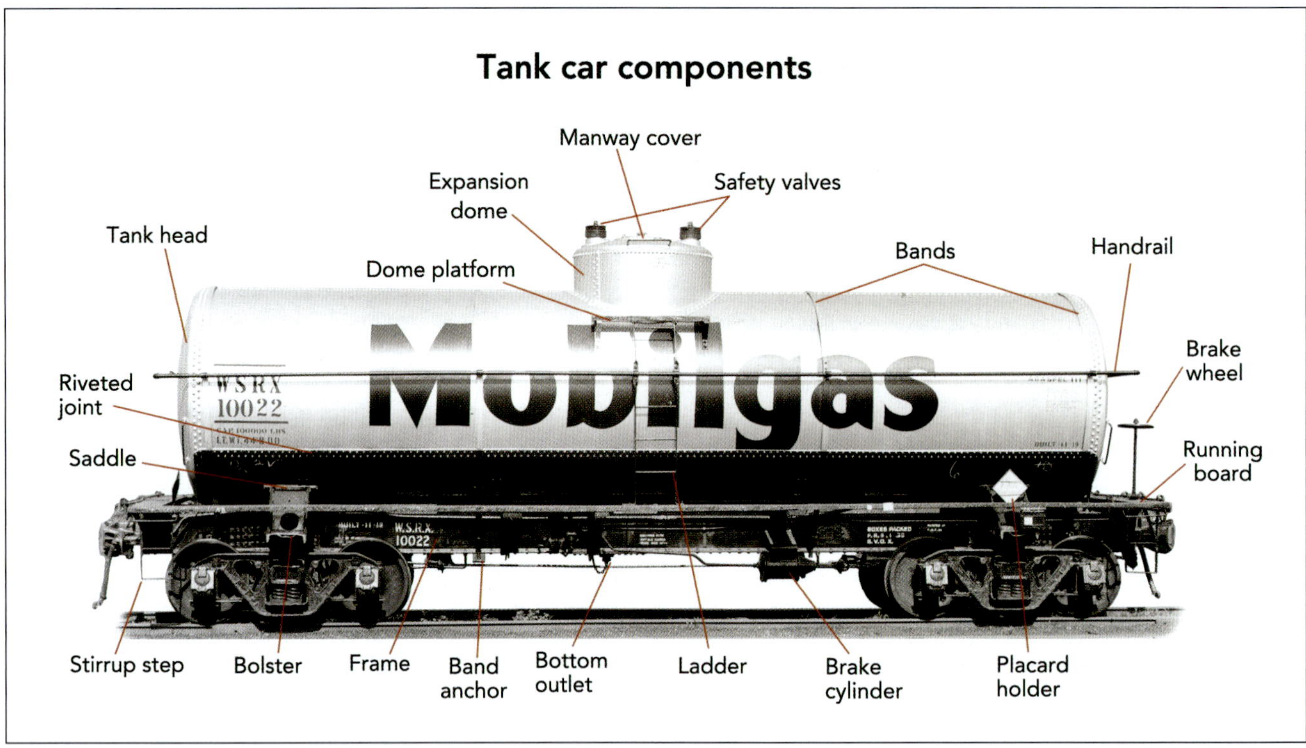

This Mobil tank car, built by Pennsylvania Tank Car, shows the major components of tank car construction after the adaptation of MCB 1917 standards. The ARA III car was built in 1919. *Jay Williams collection; Big Four Graphics*

of the 1870s and 1880s had capacities of 20 to 30 tons, so tanks were small, around 3,000 to 6,000 gallons.

As metallurgy improved, tank construction moved to steel by the 1890s. With oil production increasing and transport distances becoming longer, the oil industry began buying and leasing large numbers of these cars, with nearly 10,000 in service by 1900. Since Standard Oil controlled most oil production, it owned the majority of cars in service, most through its Union Tank Line subsidiary.

Increasing train speeds, a higher number of cars in service, and a couple of decades of experience led to improved and safer car designs. The move to "modern" tank car design began in 1903 when the Master Car Builders Association developed specifications for tank car construction; these would become standard in 1910. Cars built prior to the adopted standard were designated as Class I cars (eventually ARA I, for American Railway Association, when that

This 8,000-gallon car was built by Standard Steel Car in 1906 for Gulf. It has the basic look of a more modern car, but has full channel sideframes, heavy bulkheads ("tank head blocks") on the frame at each end of the tank to secure it, single rivet lines securing the seams along each of the five radial courses of the tank, and an offset ladder. *Standard Steel Car Co.*

Spotting features

Size characteristics (gallon capacity, tank diameter, and overall length) are the first obvious features. Look at whether a car has riveted or welded construction (and then at the rivet and weld-seam patterns), whether it is insulated, whether it is a pressure- or non-pressure car, and whether it has an underframe or is frameless with stub sills.

The bolster, tank saddle, and stub-sill designs are distinctive among manufacturers. Also check ladder locations and styles; the style, shape, and size of the expansion dome or bonnet; the style and location of safety valves; the location (or lack of) steam-heat connections; and the size, shape, and location of running boards, end platforms, and platforms and railings around the dome or bonnet.

Also check the style and design of trucks (solid- or roller-bearing). Roller-bearing trucks were required on all new 100-ton cars starting in 1963, on all new cars in 1968, and on all interchange equipment by 1995.

Check brake gear location and style. Early 1900s cars had K style brakes, with AB brakes becoming mandatory on new cars in 1932; all cars in interchange service were required to have AB brakes by 1953, and many older cars were converted. Also check the style of the brake wheel and staff on the end or end platform.

The Van Dyke design was the first frameless tank car. This 10,000-gallon version was built in 1906 for Union. Although a strong, lightweight design, it would be several decades before frameless cars would become standard. *Union Tank Car Co.*

This 10,000-gallon American Car & Foundry Type 17 car, built in 1917 to the new ARA III standards, has a single longitudinal lower course with five upper radial tank courses, all with double rivet rows. *Jay Williams collection, Big Four Graphics*

organization was formed in 1917); those built to the 1910 standard were Class II (ARA II) cars.

Car construction

You can see the typical components of a steam-era tank car in the photo on the previous page. The tank itself is formed by multiple sections ("courses") of rolled steel sheet. Early cars generally had a single longitudinal lower section with multiple cross (radial) top sections, all riveted together. Ends are slightly convex and are riveted to the tank.

Single rows of rivets were typically used at joints until the 1910s; double rows of rivets became standard in 1917. By the 1920s, construction moved to all longitudinal courses, with three or four sections depending upon tank size. Tank size varied, with 6,000- and 8,000-gallon cars the most common for that period.

Tanks featured a large dome at the top middle designed to allow expansion of the product due to heat. Without this room to expand, internal pressures can increase beyond tank capacity. Dome size was based on capacity, so larger cars had bigger domes.

The top of the dome had a hinged opening with a lid (manway) to allow filling and access.

A safety valve was attached to the dome. Early cars had this attached with an L-shaped pipe to the side of the dome; after the 1920s, the valve became part of the top of the dome.

Note that even though these are "non-pressure" cars, significant internal pressure can sometimes build up. The spring-loaded safety valve was set to release at a pressure from 75 pounds (most early cars) to, on some modern cars, 165 pounds of pressure. These are officially known as "pressure-relief devices" (Department of Transportation, Transport Canada) or "safety-relief devices" (Association of American Railroads).

The AC&F Type 21 car has a squat appearance. This 10,000-gallon ARA III car built for Tidewater has all longitudinal tank courses, and the safety valve has moved to atop the expansion dome (which still has the older screw-on style hatch cover). It was built in 1922 and photographed in 1961. *John Ingles; J. David Ingles collection*

AC&F's Type 27 car was a common steam-era design. This three-compartment ICC 103 version shows the longer frame that gives the Type 27 a sleeker appearance than the earlier Type 17 and 21 cars. The vertical rivet lines aren't tank courses, but mark the location of the internal compartment ends. *Robert A. Campbell, Sr.*

Early tank cars had separate frames, with the tank itself resting on curved saddles above the bolster at each end. A riveted anchor at the middle secured the tank to the underframe, allowing for expansion and contraction of the tank along its length. The tank was further secured by two or four straps (bands) that wrapped from the frame around the top of the tank.

General-purpose cars are loaded from the top through the opening atop the dome and unloaded through an outlet in a depressed area (sump) under the car, at the bottom of the tank. The dome hatch on early cars was a screw-on cover, but by the 1920s hatches were secured by multiple bolts around the rim of the hatch. The bottom outlet valve is controlled by a wheel at the top of the car that turns a rod extending through the interior.

The UTLX X-3 was the most common tank car of the steam and early diesel eras. This 10,000-gallon version, built in the 1920s, has longitudinal riveted tank courses, bolted manway cover, and Union's distinctive box-style end platform that extends from the bolster. *Cornelius W. Hauck*

Some cars also allow unloading from a top connection; this eduction pipe extends down through the tank interior to the bottom.

Extensions from the frame to the side supported running boards (walkways) along each side of the car, with platforms or a narrow running board along the end of the car. Tank cars were equipped with standard brake gear, couplers, and trucks.

Updated specs and standards

Tank specifications and standards were revised in 1917. The most notable visual change was that double rows of rivets were required at the tank seams. Cars built to this new standard were designated ARA III. The main structural improvement was a higher internal pressure (60 psi), with improved and heavier metal components and improved safety devices and valves. Earlier cars could continue in service carrying flammable products if they were rated at 60 psi; otherwise, they were now restricted to carrying nonhazardous liquids.

Also at that time a new car class was introduced, ARA IV, which was designed for highly volatile liquids requiring higher pressure (more on those in Chapter 6).

General American was a prolific builder of tank cars in the steam era. They can be spotted by the open construction at the ends, with the ends of the bolsters prominently in view. This 8,000-gallon ICC 103 car, owned by American Petrofina of Texas, was built in 1929 and photographed in 1964. *J. David Ingles*

In 1927 the Interstate Commerce Commission took over issuing tank car standards from the ARA, adopting three-digit numbers to distinguish car designs. Older ARA I and II cars kept those designations, while ARA III cars became ICC 103. Standards were updated, with two safety valves required on tanks larger than 6,500 gallons.

Notable designs

Unlike other freight car types that were often built to various USRA (United States Railroad Administration), ARA, or later AAR standard or recommended-practice designs, tank car design was largely left to manufacturers and car-fleet owners. Some shared common traits; distinctive spotting features among them includes the designs of the underframes, tank saddles, bolsters, and end platforms.

The major tank car builders through the steam and early diesel eras were American Car & Foundry and General American, with minor builders including Pennsylvania Tank Car Co.,

This end view of a General American insulated car shows the bolted construction of the end and side jacketing, the two end steam-line connections, the placard holder (empty), and the wood running boards. The bands (far right) pass through the jacket and insulation to secure the tank itself. *R.L. Klings collection*

Cars in liquid petroleum service have bottom outlets, with the screw-on caps secured by mounting chains. This General American car also has bottom-mounted steam-heat connections (on either side of the larger bottom outlet), with caps also secured by chains. *Jeff Wilson*

Standard Steel Car Co., Pressed Steel Car Co., and Chicago Steel Car Co.

Union Tank Car (UTLX) was the largest tank car operator, but it contracted with multiple builders for its cars, having them build cars to Union's own designs. Union continued this until acquiring Graver Tank Co. in 1957, whereupon it began building its own cars.

John Van Dyke of Union developed (and in 1903 patented) a design for a frameless design that would be named after him; although many were built into the 1910s, railroads remained skeptical of the design, and it would be another five decades before Union finally persuaded the industry that frameless cars were practical and safe.

Van Dyke altered the design to include a frame, and the result was the Union Class X car, one of the most common early designs (page 97). It is easily spotted by its running boards, which stand taller than other contemporary cars, and its horizontally mounted brake staff, which is mounted on the tank end with the brake wheel toward the side. About 7,200 Class X cars were built through the 1910s; many survived in service into the 1950s. (UTLX cars had their builder's class stenciled on the end of the car below the reporting marks — the most reliable of spotting features.)

In 1917, Union introduced its X-3 design to meet the new ARA III standards. It would become the most common tank car of the steam to early diesel eras, with more than 19,000 built into the 1940s. The tanks were built in four sizes: with 6,500-, 8,000-, 10,000-, and 12,500-gallon capacity, with the 10,000-gallon versions the most common (more than 12,000 were built). These had longitudinal courses (three on smaller cars; four on 12,500-gallon cars), four tank bands, and distinctive boxed-in bolsters and end side sills. Most had a ladder and dome platform only on one side of the car.

A word on tank sizes: Cars are usually described by their nominal capacity in gallons, but rounded to the nearest 1,000 or 500. Thus a car with a capacity of 8,162 gallons is simply called an 8,000-gallon car.

Further variations were the X-3 car sizes, with two underframes (37'-5" and 32'-2") and two tank diameters (6'-4" and 8'-7"). The 6,500-gallon cars all had the short underframe, while 8,000-gallon tanks were built in both long frame/narrow tank and short frame/wide tank versions.

The basic appearance of these cars remained constant through production, although there were many detail changes to the bolster, underframe, dome, and other details, as well as the switch from AB to K brakes in 1932 (with many earlier cars retrofitted with

AB brakes). Some could still be seen in service into the 1980s.

American Car & Foundry was a major car builder of the early 1900s. It referred to its various tank car designs by "Type," with a number based on the year it was designed. Several early versions were built, including the Type 7 (with high-mounted running boards) and Type 17 (low running boards; radial courses above a longitudinal bottom course).

A common early car, many of which survived well into the diesel era, was the AC&F Type 21, first built in 1921. These had longitudinal tank courses (three on 8,000-gallon and smaller cars, four on 10,000-gallon cars) and four tank bands. The end sills were channel-style, distinct from the Union design.

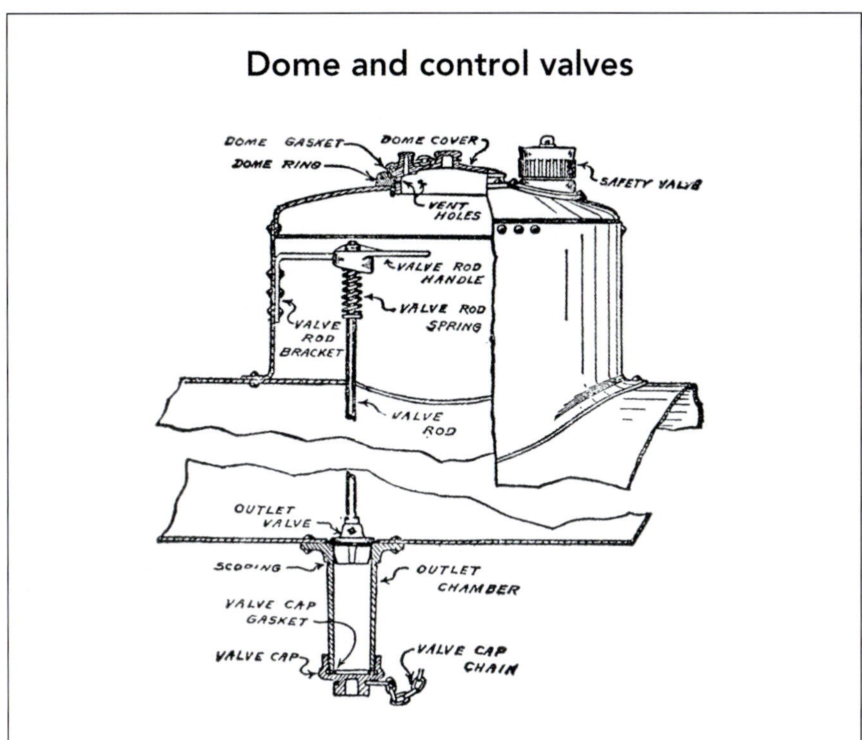

This cutaway view shows how the outlet valve is controlled at the top of the car, with a rod passing through the tank to the top of the outlet chamber under the car. This construction was standard through the 1950s. *Association of American Railroads*

Another common car was the Type 27, which came out in 1927 to meet the new ARA standards introduced that year. These were characterized by longer underframes with narrower, longer tanks, giving them a sleeker appearance compared to the earlier, "squatty" Type 21. The most common sizes of the Type 27 were the 8,000- and 10,000-gallon versions, but some 6,000- and 12,000-gallon cars were also built. These had two tank bands (at the bolsters).

The 8,000- and 10,000-gallon cars were 36 feet long, the 6,000-gallon version was 32 feet, and the 12,000-gallon car was 39 feet long.

The other major builder was General American, which began as German American but changed its name in 1916. Its early cars, through World War I, had two tank anchors to the underframe. Its most common late-steam-era car was the Type 30, spotted by its lack of an end sill, with large bolsters and the tank saddle visible at each end. Tanks of 8,000 and 10,000 gallons were most common, with some 6,000- and 12,500-gallon cars.

Insulated and heated cars

Most general-purpose cars are non-insulated. The outer shell you see is the outside of the tank itself. Some

Warren Petroleum was a major tank car operator, with more than 6,000 cars in service by the early 1960s. This is an insulated 8,000-gallon ARA IV car, typically used for volatile casing-head gas. *Trains magazine collection*

The Barrett Company was a major tank car operator into the 1940s, with more than 1,400 cars for carrying its Tarvia asphalt products. This insulated 10,000-gallon car (note the lip of the outer shell around the end), built by AC&F, has steam-heating coils. *Trains magazine collection*

tank cars are insulated, with a layer of insulating material over the tank, covered by a thin outer steel jacket or shell. A tell-tale sign for this is the bands, which pass through a hole in the jacketing.

Some cars are heated, meaning they have steam-heat coils either inside the tank itself (internal) or on the outside of the tank, but under an outer jacket (external). These have a pair of external pipe couplings on the end or under the car that are connected to a steam source at the receiving dock. This is done to make high-viscosity liquids flow more readily; examples include No. 6 fuel oil (Bunker C), tar, and other heavy oils.

Cars may be non-insulated but heated (internal only), or insulated with or without heating coils.

Multi-compartment cars

Although the majority of cars have a single tank, some were built with multiple compartments. Three was most common for petroleum cars. In the steam and early diesel eras, when railroads were a primary supplier for local fuel dealers, multiple compartments were handy for shipping multiple products (different grades of gasoline, for example) with a single car. Compartments could be of equal or different sizes, with the capacity stenciled on the dome above each compartment. Dome size is based on the capacity of its compartment, not the entire car.

Each compartment is required to have its own tank heads, convex to the compartment, with an air gap between them (adjoining compartments don't share a common tank head). You can spot this on riveted cars by the radial rivet lines that mark the location of each head.

Remember that with a multi-compartment tank, each compartment will need a separate hazmat placard for the product it's carrying.

This 10,000-gallon UTLX class Z car has two compartments: one large (6,556 gallons) and one small (3,292), with expansion-dome size reflecting the compartment size differences. It was built by Standard Tank Car in 1932. *Trains magazine collection*

Pressed Steel Car Co. built this 8,000-gallon, three-compartment tank car for Deep Rock in 1930. The center compartment is 4,000 gallons and the other compartments are each 2,000 gallons, although each has identical domes.
Trains Magazine collection

Welded cars

High-pressure tank cars (see Chapter 6) had been built with welded tanks since their development in the late 1920s, necessitated by the strength required to contain products under pressure. Non-pressure cars continued to be riveted, as it was still a more economical process than welding.

By the late 1940s, however, automated fusion welding techniques were becoming more advanced. Welding was becoming more cost-efficient than riveting (which was extremely labor-intensive), and welded bodies began appearing on general-purpose cars. Few riveted tank cars were built after the late 1940s, but not many welded ones appeared simply because few new petroleum cars would be built for the next decade.

The end of World War II marked the start of a sharp decline in petroleum traffic by rail, with the expansion of pipelines and the loss of wartime traffic. Even with the rise in domestic gasoline use with wartime restrictions ended, shippers were able to handle the traffic with existing cars, retiring the oldest (particularly ARA I and II cars) that had served through the war.

The new welded general-purpose tank cars initially looked much like the older riveted cars as far as design, but with raised welded seams instead of rows of rivets. The ICC class remained the same, but with a W suffix (e.g., ICC 103W). Among the biggest buyers of these cars were railroads (for company fuel and oil service) and the Department of Defense (delivering fuel to military installations).

Modern cars

The true start of the modern tank car era came with the adoption of the frameless tank car, which eliminated the separate underframe. On a frameless car, the tank is welded directly to a stub sill at each end. The tank itself then provides the structural strength to transmit train forces. Although Union had done this with the Van Dyke car back in the early 1900s, it wasn't widely accepted until the company reintroduced the style with its all-welded "hot dog" car in 1954. It still took several years of testing before the ICC approved the design in 1961.

By the early 1960s, welded frameless construction had become the standard for most new cars. The elimination of the underframe was a distinctive, easy-to-spot feature.

The other distinct change was the elimination of the expansion dome. Instead, shippers were to allow room inside the tank itself for expansion (1% or 2% for most products; 5% for products poisonous by inhalation). Replacing the dome was a smaller bonnet covering control valves, with a separate small manway and safety valve.

The approval of domeless cars created ICC classes 111 (non-pressure) and 112 (pressure). Designations now also included tank test pressure and construction. For example, an ICC 111A 60W is a tank without expansion dome, fusion welded, with a test pressure of 60 psi (the A is a delineator letter without meaning). In 1967 the Department of Transportation took over specification duties, with a "DOT" prefix replacing the ICC.

Another change by the early 1960s was the elimination of side running boards, just as running boards were being eliminated from boxcars and other car types. Replacing them was a long safety railing running the length of the car between bolsters, designed to keep people from getting too close to the car and tracks.

Tank car sizes also began increasing dramatically by the 1960s as the industry moved from the 50-ton cars of the steam and early diesel eras to 70-ton cars by the late 1950s and 100-ton cars in the early 1960s. For liquid petroleum cars, this meant tanks of 20,000 gallons by the early 1960s and 25,000-gallon and larger cars by the late 1960s.

By the late 1950s, tank car size was growing to match increases in allowable weight (gross rail load) regulations. ACF built this 20,000-gallon ICC 111A 100W1 (domeless, welded, 100-psi pressure) car in December 1958. It has roller-bearing trucks, but still has a separate underframe. *ACF Industries*

On domeless non-pressure cars, the top features a separate manway/hatch (left) and a bonnet that holds control valves. Lettering on the railing at left calls out the amount of top space needed for 2% outage; lettering on the body reminds workers to vent the tank when unloading. *Cody Grivno*

In 1967 Union introduced a distinctive new tank car design called the Funnel-Flow. Both ends of its cylindrical tank slope downward toward the middle to allow loads to empty more completely than conventional cars. Other builders soon produced their own variations of the design, usually simply termed "sloped-bottom" cars. They have been made in a wide variety of sizes and slope angles for different commodities; they are sometimes used in liquid petroleum service.

By the late 1960s manufacturers had built several huge tank cars (mainly for chemicals, but some for LPG) ranging to 50,000 gallons (see Chapter 6). In November 1970 the DOT limited tank car size at 34,500 gallons and 100-ton (263,000-pound gross rail load) capacity.

The most common cars in petroleum service today are 23,600-gallon general-service tank cars, which can be used for fuel oil (heavier petroleum products), and larger 26,000- to 30,000-gallon cars used for lighter-density products like gasoline and ethanol (shipped by rail to many tank terminals for blending with gasoline).

The major builders today include Union, Greenbrier (Gunderson), and Trinity (which purchased General American in 1984); others in the modern era include ARI (the former railcar division of ACF Industries), Richmond Tank Car (until 1983), and North American (until 1985).

Safety issues stemming from accidents involving DOT 111 cars led to a new DOT 117 specification for tank cars. Cars built after October 2015 are required to follow these updated specs; older DOT 111 cars are being removed from service (or reassigned and refitted to carry non-hazardous commodities), with a target date of 2025.

Characteristics of the new design are a thicker tank shell (9⁄16" as opposed to the 7⁄16" of DOT 111 cars), heavier full-height head shields (½"), thermal insulation with a steel exterior

This UTLX car, built in 1960, has a 20,000-gallon capacity and is a welded, non-insulated, frameless car without an expansion dome. It's leased to Sunoco. *John Ingles; J. David Ingles collection*

jacket, and improved designs for top fittings and valves and bottom outlets and handles to make them more resistant to damage and product release in accidents.

Unlike the steam era, where the vast majority of tank cars were in petroleum service, modern general-service cars carry a tremendous variety of products. With the lack of corporate logos and lettering, often the only way to identify what a car is hauling is to check placards.

As of 2022, there were 443,800 tank cars in service; 200,700 were DOT 111 cars, the largest group. The next-largest group were the new DOT 117 cars (87,600). General-service cars greatly outnumber pressure cars.

Car capacity data and Plate designations

Car capacity for freight cars is generally described by the approximate load it can carry in tons. For tank cars, a more descriptive identifier is usually the tank capacity in gallons. The true limit for cars is their gross rail load (GRL), which is the total weight of the car itself plus its load allowed on the rails. Through the steam and early diesel eras, most were 50-ton cars (169,000-pound, or 169K GRL), with some older cars at 40 tons (GRL of 136,000 pounds).

By the late 1950s, 70-ton cars were allowed on most routes (210K GRL), and in 1963 the AAR updated those limits, at the same time making 100-ton cars the standard for interchange (263K GRL). In 1995 the GRL limit was bumped to 110 tons (286K GRL), but tank cars carrying many types of hazardous products are limited to 263K. These increased weight limits are the reason tank car sizes expanded significantly from the late 1950s into the 1970s.

Along with weight, cars are limited by size in various dimensions. These are stated by outline drawings known as "Plates." The first of these, Plate B, was established in 1948, followed by Plate C in 1963, which allows slightly taller height than Plate B. Cars matching Plate B have no identifying lettering; since the early 1970s, cars above Plate B but within Plate C carry a simple "Plate C" stencil.

Shelf couplers and head shields

With the move to larger cars in the 1960s, safety considerations became more important. Shelf-style couplers were required on new tank cars carrying hazardous cargo beginning in 1970. This was expanded to include all tank cars in 1975, with older cars to be retrofitted by 1979. These are designed to keep couplers in alignment in derailments, helping keep cars upright as well as keeping couplers from separating and then puncturing the end of the neighboring tank car in a wreck.

Another move to improve safety is the requirement for thicker head shields on car ends, again to reduce the chance of a coupler or other piece of debris puncturing the tank in a wreck. Head shields were required on new cars and had to be retrofitted to older cars by December 1979. These could be separate or integrated to the car end (as done for new construction). Retrofitted

Union developed its Funnel Flow design in 1967, featuring a tank that angles down toward the middle. Other manufacturers soon followed with similar designs. This DOT 111A 100W3 car is shown in 2004. *Jeff Wilson*

cars with separate head shields have a distinctive appearance (see page 93 for a pressure car with a retrofitted shield).

TankTrain cars

An innovative tank car design was introduced by General American in 1977. Called TankTrain, it's a multi-car system with individual cars connected by flexible 10"-diameter hoses. Up to 15 cars can be connected in a string, with each group of cars loaded and unloaded from just one end car. Loading is at the rate of up to 3,000 gallons per minute; a five-car string can be loaded in about 90 minutes.

The first were 23,500-gallon, insulated cars often used in oil and petroleum-product service; other sizes and variations were later built. The first of these were black with prominent "TankTrain" lettering; later cars simply had the reporting marks and data. (See the photo on the next page.) Most were operated as part of General American's GATX leasing fleet.

Some operators ran multiple sets of TankTrain cars as unit trains; others shipped smaller cuts of cars that were handled in standard manifest freight trains. Most were out of service by the 2020s.

Tank car ownership, fleets

Tank cars historically have not been owned by railroads, but instead by private owners (individual shippers or leasing companies). Railroads have always desired cars that can be used for multiple kinds of loads (boxcars, flatcars, gondolas), so that when one load is emptied, the car is immediately ready for the next. With tank cars, though, loads are highly specialized—a tank car carrying crude oil, for example, cannot then be used for a load of vegetable oil, and then for a load of sulfuric acid. This meant that most tank cars spent half their time empty.

This 26,000-gallon general-purpose car was in Sunoco's 800-car fleet in 1976. The DOT 111A 100W1 car was built by General American. *J. David Ingles*

Another example of a car featuring prominent lettering of its lessee is this Quaker State car, built by General American and shown in 1984. It's a four-compartment, non-insulated DOT 111A 100W1 car. *J. David Ingles collection*

General American introduced its TankTrain car design in 1977. These cars could be connected by flexible hoses on each end, allowing multiple cars to be loaded and unloaded from a single point. These 26,000-gallon cars, built in 1980, are carrying gasoline for lessee Global Partners on Vermont Ry. in June 2014. *Scott A. Hartley*

The result was the growth of leasing companies. As with the oil business itself, more than half of the tank cars in service in the early 1900s were owned and controlled by John D. Rockefeller's Standard Oil Co., through Union Tank Line, which Rockefeller acquired in 1873 (originally the Star Tank Line). After the breakup of Standard in 1911, the company, renamed Union Tank Car Co. (UTLX reporting marks), became an independent company and would continue as the major owner of tank cars in North America through the 1900s. It leased cars on long- and short-term agreements to hundreds of users in the petroleum industry as well as other businesses.

The two other major tank car leasing companies through the mid-1900s included General American (GATX), which also built cars, and Shipper's Car Line (SHPX), owned by carbuilder American Car & Foundry (which later became ACF Industries). Many smaller companies also leased cars, including California Despatch Line, Crystal Car Line, and Harbor Tank Line.

By the mid-1920s, there were about 138,000 tank cars in service, of which railroads owned just over 13,000.

The largest leasing companies today are Union, General American (which no longer builds cars, but operates as a leasing company), Trinity (TILX), Greenbrier (GBRX), and GE Railcar (the former North American fleet).

The chart on page 83 lists the largest tank car fleets from 1930 to the 2020s.

Trinity built this 26,500-gallon insulated DOT 111 car, and it's carrying gasoline in this 2018 view. The jacketing is recessed on the side behind the ladder to maintain Plate C clearance. *Cody Grivno*

It shows major private owners such as Sinclair and Warren. It's important to note that many oil companies leased even larger numbers of cars from UTLX and others, and some companies both owned and leased cars. Some initially owned cars, but sold them to leasing companies and then leased them back (notably Gulf, Phillips, and Texaco). Today, almost all tank cars in petroleum service are leased by shippers.

Railroads did, and still do, own their own tank cars (substantial fleets of them in the steam era), but they were used in company service for locomotive fuel, lube oil, and water. Especially in the steam era, some railroads—notably Santa Fe and Southern Pacific, which each rostered more than 2,500—had to transport solid trains of water into desert areas for steam locomotives.

Tank car painting and lettering

Model manufacturers have a long history of painting their tank car models in bright, colorful schemes. Although many of these did exist in real life, they were in the minority. Petroleum-service cars—especially non-pressure cars—were most often painted basic black with minimal lettering. The UTLX fleet, for example, was mostly black with yellow lettering, and the GATX and SHPX fleets were primarily black with white lettering.

Large logos or company lettering were fairly common for petroleum shippers through the 1940s, and although some modern cars could be found carrying logos into the 1970s, the practice became quite rare by the late 1960s. More common is small stenciling that indicates the company leasing the car.

Some exceptions to this were Warren Petroleum, which had cars painted gray on their upper bodies with black lower bodies, green domes, and large "Warren" lettering; and Texaco, which had some early cars painted silver with large lettering. Some modern crude oil and product cars are white, but with simple black lettering.

Required lettering and stenciling on tank cars includes the reporting marks and number (on the left side). Reporting marks are assigned by the AAR; marks on privately owned cars, such as those owned by oil companies or leasing firms, end in "X." Some cars have reporting marks and other information stenciled on the top of the tank as well.

Below the reporting marks are the capacity and light weight (in pounds). Fees for tank car shipments, unlike other types of freight cars, are not based on weight but on capacity in gallons, so there's no "weight limit" line on tank cars.

On the right side of each end is the ARA, ICC, or DOT car class (or TC for Transport Canada, the Canadian issuing body); specific commodity stencil (required for some commodities if the car carries a single product—see Chapter 6 for several examples); safety valve test pressure (and date and location it was checked); and date built, with manufacturer initials.

Since 1998, cars carrying hazardous or dangerous materials are subject to periodic requalification and tests. They are marked with a matrix that includes data on various required tests, including location of testing, the date the last test was done, and when the next test is due. These include a tank thickness test, service equipment (loading/unloading fixtures), pressure-relief device, interior heating coils (if equipped), and car lining, if equipped. (A "PP" designation indicates a lining is for product purity, not to protect the tank from corrosion; these do not require requalification).

This 30,000-gallon, non-insulated Trinity-built DOT 111 car is carrying ethanol in 2006. Ethanol became a common additive to gasoline in the 2000s, and since it presents difficulties in transporting by pipeline, railcars are the common delivery method to tank terminals. *Jeff Wilson*

Gunderson built this 29,000-gallon insulated DOT 111S 100W car in 2014. It's in crude oil service in 2015. *Cody Grivno*

On cars with frames, the side of the frame will show the reporting marks and number. Toward the right will be information on the last time the journal boxes were repacked and the initials of the station and railroad doing the service.

On each tank end are the reporting marks and number, tank capacity in gallons (and liters on modern cars), and any specific details on car equipment such as type of draft gear, brake shoes, couplers, and heating coils.

Tank cars have placard holders on each side and end. These hold the familiar diamond-shaped hazardous materials placards, required when cars are loaded. Through 1975 these were generic in nature, often with "dangerous" or "hazardous" lettering. Since 1975, the DOT has adopted the four-digit UN commodity code for specific products, with the background colors indicating product characteristics (gasoline, for example, is No. 1203 on a red background, indicating a flammable product; a small "3" at the bottom indicates a Class 3 product). Other common related products include crude oil (1267) and ethanol (1987).

Since the 1970s, cars carrying hazardous materials have a decal

The new DOT 117 car, a redesigned and improved version over the DOT 111, has improved insulation, heavier shell and end shields, and tougher fittings. This 30,000-gallon car was built by Greenbrier and is on display at a trade show in 2015. *Jim Wrinn*

on each side listing an 800 phone number to report spills, fires, and other emergencies.

On older cars with expansion domes, a diamond-shaped stencil on the side of the dome indicated bolted-on hatch covers, which replaced earlier screw-on covers in the 1920s. Bolted covers are safer, as they allow workers to slowly release internal pressure, whereas screw-on covers could release pressure suddenly.

Reflective striping became mandatory on all new freight cars as of 2005 and was to be applied to all cars by 2015 (a minimum of 3.5 square feet on each side). Some cars carried reflective striping well before the legal requirement was issued.

Other lettering details match other freight cars, including consolidated stencils (starting in 1972) and Automatic Car Identification (ACI) plates. (The latter was a colored bar code that was used by trackside readers from 1967 to 1977, although many cars kept their plates for years after ACI was discontinued.) Since 1994, each car must carry an Automatic Equipment Identification (AEI) tag on each side, placed to the far right, on or near the bolster on tank cars). These small boxes house radio transponders that are read by trackside scanners.

As of 2003, new cars have a small stainless-steel plate on each side at the bolster web. The plate includes the manufacturer, serial number, date built, and car specification.

MODELING TIPS

Ready-to-run tank cars and car kits are available for a wide range of prototype cars and paint schemes. Along with plastic versions from various model railroad manufacturers, be sure to check the offerings of resin-car manufacturers, including out-of-production kits. Sunshine Models, for example, released a number of common steam-era tank car kits in HO. Also be sure to check the offerings of 3-D printed models from Shapeways.com and others.

Be sure to consider era when modeling for appropriate cars. A positive is that tank cars tended to be durable and last a long time in service, so you can often find cars approaching 40 years old still in revenue service. Also consider paint schemes. Most oil company owned and leased cars were basic black, and cars with fancy schemes and lettering were in the minority. Cars of almost any owner can pass by on through freights, but the cars you're spotting at a local fuel dealer should match the brand handled by the dealer. Let the prototype be your guide.

Tank car major owners by year

Owner	1930	1947	1962	1971	1978	2000	2020
Canadian Genl. Transit [1]	—	2,200	4,100	5,500	5,800	5,100	4,000
Cities Service [2]	260	1,500	1,800	890	970	230	100
Continental Oil Co.	1,700	900	680	1,800	890	—	—
General American (GATX)	12,100	37,400	52,100	53,200	51,200	63,500	84,200
GE Railcar Services [3]	—	—	—	—	—	37,800	—
Greenbrier Leasing	—	—	—	—	—	—	23,900
Gulf	2,100	1,500	—	1,900	1,000	—	—
Mid-Continent	2,200	1,600	—	—	—	—	—
Mobil [4]	—	—	2,100	1,100	870	2,500	14,900
North American [3]	3,300	4,500	7,100	10,400	16,500	—	—
Phillips Petroleum	2,200	670	3,600	2,900	2,100	3,100	3,900
Procor [5]	—	—	—	—	2,100	12,700	29,900
Pure Oil Co.	2,600	—	—	—	—	—	—
Shell Oil Co.	3,200	3,000	920	1,500	1,500	1,400	1,200
Shippers Car Line (SHPX) [6]	2,200	9,200	18,500	23,200	21,800	1,600	—
Sinclair	5,400	6,100	—	—	—	—	—
Socony-Vacuum [4]	—	2,500	—	—	—	—	—
Texas Co. [7]	6,800	3,900	1,900	1,300	540	—	—
Tide Water Associated	—	1,400	1,000	—	—	—	—
Trinity Leasing	—	—	—	—	—	5,100	101,500
Union Tank Car (UTLX) [5]	34,100	38,800	51,700	48,200	46,300	60,300	104,100
Warren Petroleum	170	870	6,000	—	—	—	—

1. Became GATX Rail Canada Corp. in 1996.
2. Now Citgo.
3. The North American fleet was merged into GE Railcar Services in 1985. In 2015 it was sold to Marmon Holdings; the fleet is now managed by UTLX/Procor.
4. Socony-Vacuum became Socony-Mobil in 1955 and Mobil Oil Corp. in 1966; in 1988 it merged with Exxon to become Exxon-Mobil.
5. Procor (a Canadian subsidiary of UTLX) cars are included in UTLX totals through 1971.
6. Most of the Shippers Car Line fleet was acquired by GE Railcar in 1997.
7. Texas Co. (Texaco) in 1936 sold its cars to General American and leased them back; after that date their numbers are also included in General American's roster.

CHAPTER SIX

LPG tank cars

Manufactured in 1927 by American Car & Foundry, this Phillips car is one of the first LPG cars built. The 11,000-gallon car was still in service in this 1966 image. It's an ICC 105A 100 car, with a forge-welded tank. The white streaks are from oxidation of the lettering. *Jeff Wilson collection*

The late-1920s growth of propane and butane (collectively known as liquefied petroleum gas, or LPG) as popular home-heating fuels, especially for customers in rural areas, required development of high-pressure welded tank cars. It's a traffic source that has expanded to many industries and continues for railroads today, with larger, modernized tank cars.

General American built this 11,000-gallon pressure car in 1955. The ICC 105A 300W car is carrying LPG for Union Texas Natural Gas Corp., a division of Allied Chemical. *J. David Ingles*

Although propane and butane are gases at normal atmospheric pressure, they're easily compressed to liquids at room temperature at fairly low pressures (around 100 psi). This makes LPG practical to store and transport in liquid form, and since LPG is difficult to ship by pipeline, railroads remain a key shipper of the product.

Along with fuel, LPG has found a number of other industrial uses, including as a propellent and as a feedstock (raw material) in the petrochemical industry to make a variety of other products, including plastics, rubber, and pharmaceuticals.

As Chapter 2 explains, the LPG market began growing quickly in the early 1930s, when Phillips began marketing it as a clean-burning home heating fuel (calling its version Philgas). Other companies soon followed; Skelly Oil called its product Skelgas, Pure Oil Co. had Puregas, and generic names included "bottle gas" or "home gas." Soon LPG was being sold by many refining companies across the country, especially in colder climates. Sales of LPG went from 4 million gallons in 1928 to more than 220 million gallons per year by the late 1930s.

As Chapter 3 highlighted, many local LPG dealers also did installation and maintenance on gas furnaces and kitchen appliances, including selling branded appliances, which helped assure the oil companies a growing base of loyal customers for their LPG sales.

Early LPG cars

The initial challenge was efficiently getting LPG from refineries to local dealers. The first rail transport of liquid propane was in 1927, using individual storage containers loaded aboard a flatcar. This proved cumbersome, and tank cars would soon follow.

Tank cars carrying LPG differ considerably from the general-purpose, non-pressure cars used for liquid petroleum products. Pressure cars for LPG have welded instead of riveted seams, with thicker steel shells than non-pressure cars to withstand the forces of the compressed gas. The

The bonnet on a pressure car houses the valves and connections for the two product lines (longitudinal to the car), the air/vent line (side), and the safety valve (center of bonnet). *Russell Lee, Library of Congress*

first forge-welded tanks appeared in 1920, with a move to fusion-welding for pressure tanks in the 1930s. Forge welding (lap welding) involved overlaying adjoining sheets of red-hot steel, then using hammer blows to join the mating surfaces. It was the only practical method for welding large tanks through the 1920s.

The fusion welding process, which involves using intense heat (gas flame or electric arc) at a joint to melt parts together, grew in popularity and reliability by the mid-1930s. An issue was that the intense heat at narrow locations caused stresses in the metal because of uneven expansion and contraction; this could lead to cracking or failure of a tank under pressure. The solution came when car builders acquired annealing ovens big enough to hold an entire tank to even the stresses of heat from the process. Both ACF and General American, the major builders of these cars into the 1950s, had this capability by the 1930s.

Pressure cars lack bottom outlets and don't have expansion domes. Instead, a top bonnet covers the loading and unloading connections (two liquid product lines, pointing to the ends of the car, and one for vapor, pointing to the side of the car) and valves, as well as the safety valve. The photo above shows the fittings of a typical pressure car.

Starting in 1927, following the then-new ICC standards for tank cars, cars designed for high pressure were designated class 105. This class replaced the old ARA V designation for pressure cars. The new ICC designations also included the test pressure of the car in pounds per square inch (psi) and the construction method. Thus an ICC 105A 300W was a Class 105 car with a test pressure of 300 psi; the W signifies a fusion-welded tank. The ICC 105A 100 on page 84 is a Class 105 car with a forge-welded tank and a test pressure of 100 psi.

These cars were jacketed, with a thin layer of insulation (usually cork) and an outer thin steel sheathing. This wasn't to insulate the product, but to protect

This pressure car was built by Graber for UTLX in 1955 and leased to Tuloma Gas. *John Ingles; J. David Ingles collection*

Construction styles began changing by the late 1950s. ACF built this 11,000-gallon LPG car for Phillips in 1957. It's an ICC 112A 400W, lacking insulation and the customary jacketing with the overlapping lip on the ends of earlier ICC 105 cars. *ACF Industries*

These Warren LPG tanks, shown at McCook, Neb., in 1968, are 11,000-gallon, ICC 105A 300W cars. Built by ACF, their construction style is similar to the 112A car in the top photo, but although these cars are insulated, the end jacketing is rounded. *Jim Seacrest*

This 30,000-gallon ICC 112A 400W car, built by Union in April 1960 and leased to Tuloma Gas, was proudly lettered as the "world's largest tank car" when built (left). By 1964, it was just another grimy (but still large) LPG car (top), with its status lettering (except the "W") painted out, as car sizes were growing rapidly. *Above: J. David Ingles; Left: Union Tank Car Co.*

it from heat if the car was exposed to a fire in an accident. The jacketing gives these early cars a distinct appearance, with a noticeable lip where the side jacketing overlaps the ends.

The welding process, heavier shell, specialized fittings, and jacketing all meant pressure cars were expensive to build compared to general-service tank cars. Their total numbers remained fairly small through the 1930s as the Depression slowed the switch from coal to gas and oil furnaces. The cars began being built in larger numbers when the LPG market began growing significantly in the 1940s, especially following World War II.

The first generation of LPG cars, built from the late 1920s into the early 1950s, had tanks from 10,500-11,000 gallons. They were larger than most contemporary non-pressure petroleum cars, as LPG is a lightweight, low-density product compared to other products. LPG weighs just over 4 pounds per gallon, compared to 6 pounds per gallon for gasoline, about 7 pounds per gallon for lube oil, and 7 to 8 pounds per gallon for crude oil.

Many, but not all, of these cars have platforms with handrails surrounding the bonnet atop the car. This is largely by preference of the owner or lessee to suit their particular loading and unloading racks.

Common early designs for LPG cars were the AC&F Type 27, in 10,500-gallon (37 feet long) and 11,000-gallon (39-foot) versions. General American and Union also built and operated similar cars; they differed slightly in tank styles and had bolster details that matched their non-pressure cars.

Nearly identical cars were built through this period for anhydrous ammonia service. Similar but significantly smaller pressure cars were built for other products, namely tetraethyl lead (see page 90) and chlorine.

Many petroleum companies in this period owned their own cars or leased fleets from Union and others; some carried company names in bold lettering and logos, as with other early non-pressure cars. Many of these cars remained in service through the 1970s.

Modern pressure cars

An increase in car weight limits in the late 1950s allowed pressure-car capacity to grow, with 70-ton cars

Union kept stretching its single-diameter car design. This is one of three 38,500-gallon LPG cars UTLX built for lease to Atlantic Refining Co. in late 1960. *Union Tank Car Co.*

ACF built its first multi-diameter ("whalebelly") pressure car in 1962, dubbing it the "Rail King 30." The first had a 30,800-gallon capacity. *ACF Industries*

Tetraethyl lead cars

Tetraethyl lead (TEL) was a common additive to gasoline, used as an octane booster, from the early 1920s into the 1970s. The Ethyl Corporation, founded by Standard Oil in 1921, was the major supplier, but DuPont and others produced it, as well.

Because TEL is a very volatile product, transporting it required pressure cars, like LPG. But since tetraethyl lead is about 14 pounds per gallon in liquid form (more than three times the density of LPG), the cars used to carry it were much smaller. Typical sizes of TEL cars through the steam and early diesel eras ranged from 3,000 to 6,000 gallons, giving these cars a distinct, diminutive appearance compared to cars carrying LPG. They would often be found at refineries.

The Ethyl Corp. had a significant fleet of cars (780 in 1962, plus another 50 cars for Ethyl Corp. of Canada, plus leased cars), and they wore versions of a light-colored scheme with the company name and logo.

The elimination of lead from automotive fuel in 1973 (starting with 1975-model cars) dramatically reduced the need for TEL after that point, although it is still used in some types of fuel (notably aviation gasoline).

General American built this 3,100-gallon, ICC 105A 300W car for the Ethyl Corp. in 1948; it's shown in 1966. The stenciling at right reads "FOR MOTOR FUEL ANTIKNOCK COMPOUND ONLY." *John Ingles; J. David Ingles collection*

As with LPG cars, TEL cars grew larger as weight limits increased. This ICC 105A 300W car, built by ACF in 1966, has a 10,000-gallon capacity. *J. David Ingles*

General American built this 6,000-gallon tank car for DuPont for tetraethyl lead service in 1958. *J. David Ingles*

General American built this multi-diameter 32,000-gallon pressure car; it was rolling through Topeka, Kan., in 1971 lettered for Gulf (which had merged with Warren, whose reporting marks are on the car). *J. David Ingles collection*

This 33,000-gallon multi-diameter ICC 112A 340W car, built by ACF for its SHPX lease fleet in 1964, is carrying an LPG load in 1967. Note the different saddles and ends compared to the General American car in the top photo. *J. David Ingles*

Richmond Tank Car built this this 28,500-gallon, 112A 340W car in 1970 for Union Tank Car's leasing fleet. The single-diameter tank has elliptical ends. *J. David Ingles*

Some multi-diameter cars served into the 2000s, like this PLM International car in 2002. For a period in the 1980s, a Canadian Transport regulation required a red horizontal stripe on cars carrying hazardous products. The rule was not adopted by the U.S. and was soon dropped for Canadian cars, but many remained painted this way for years. *J. David Ingles*

becoming more common. As with non-pressure cars, by the early 1960s high-pressure cars were also moving to frameless designs.

Pressure cars of conventional design, but up to 15,000-gallon capacity, were being built by 1960, with some LPG cars moving to non-jacketed (ICC 112 class) construction. These could be spotted by their rounded ends, as they lacked the overlap of exterior jacketing material.

With the adoption of 100-ton cars (263,000 pounds gross rail load) as standard for interchange in 1963, LPG tank car size increased dramatically compared to the 50-ton cars of the steam and early diesel eras. For pressure cars of the period, this meant two basic frameless designs. Some featured longer, single-diameter tanks to 26,000 gallon and higher capacity, or multi-diameter tanks of around 30,000 gallons in size.

The multi-diameter tanks, nicknamed "whalebelly" cars, were narrow in diameter at the ends above the trucks, but became wider and tapered downward between the trucks. This increased capacity while keeping

Union built this single-diameter 28,000-gallon car for Canadian subsidiary Procor in 1973. The DOT 112A 340W car was leased to Canadian company Dome Gas Corp. in 1976. *J. David Ingles*

Shelf-style couplers have been required on new tank cars since 1979. They help keep cars aligned in derailments and accidents. *Jeff Wilson*

Tank car construction standards were raised in the late 1970s, and older tank cars without head shields were retrofitted with external (shown here) head shields or new head shields directly on the tank. This shield, weighing about 800 pounds, has been added to a DOT 112 pressure car in 1978. *Railway Progress Institute*

the overall car length shorter and keeping it within Plate C clearance limits. The General American car on page 91, for example, has a 99" diameter at the ends and is 118" in the middle. The top of the car is level, with gradual tapers expanding on the sides and bottom.

Most of these cars of both designs had car-length top running boards with handrails on the roof and a ladder on each end.

The late 1960s saw the construction of a flurry of super-size tank cars, mainly for chemicals but some for LPG. These ranged from 36,000 to 50,000 gallons and were up to 94 feet long. Some had a 125-ton (315,000-pound GRL) capacity and rode on either six-wheel trucks or pairs of four-wheel trucks, two at each end.

In November 1970 the DOT limited tank car size at 34,500 gallons and 100-ton (263K GRL) capacity, but a few oversized cars operated into the 2000s. No multi-diameter tank cars were built after that period, but some of them ran into the 2000s, as well.

After 1970, the trend in LPG cars was a wider-diameter (108"-119"),

Trinity built this 33,600-gallon Plate C car in 1996. The jacketed DOT 112J 340W car is carrying non-odorized LPG on the BNSF in Minnesota in 2016. *Jeff Wilson*

This 33,600-gallon, DOT 112J 400W car was built by General American. The jacketing on the side is recessed to keep it within Plate C clearance specifications. *Cody Grivno*

This ARI-built pressure car has side ladders, but they're offset toward the ends to conform to Plate C. The car is carrying non-odorized LPG in 2016. *Jeff Wilson*

long tank with constant diameter; most cars are 65 feet long. To keep the cars in Plate C clearance, the ladders are located either on the ends or on each side, but toward the end (just inside the truck). On insulated/jacketed pressure cars, there is sometimes a notch or indentation in the jacketing along the sides to keep the clearance width at the middle of the car within the limit.

Although the late 1950s and later saw a huge growth in the number of pressure cars used for a variety of chemicals and other products, LPG cars are generally easy to spot because of their large size. The other common product that travels in nearly identical cars is anhydrous ammonia. To tell the difference, look for the product stenciling at the right of each side and at the hazmat placards.

Tank specifications were taken over by the Department of Transportation in 1967, so "DOT" replaced "ICC" in the classification line. Most modern LPG cars are classes 105A300W, 105J300W, 105J400W, 112J340W, and 112J400W. The "J" indicates jacketed thermal protection, which has been required for cars carrying flammable materials since 1980.

Shelf-style couplers have been required on cars built since 1979 and had to be retrofitted to older cars by 1982. Head shields were required to be retrofitted on all cars not built with them by December 1979. Retrofitted head shields could be external (as on the car on page 93) or internal, built into the tank end.

Modern cars have been built by Union, General American, ACF (and ARI, the current car-building division of ACF), Trinity, and Greenbrier; many carry the reporting marks of those companies' leasing divisions. Many have similar appearances, but the best spotting feature is the end sills and tank saddles. See Chapter 5 for details on spotting.

Pressure cars remain in the minority in the tank car fleet, but there are still plenty of them out there. Of the 443,000-plus tank cars in service as of 2022, 62,836 were DOT 112 cars and 22,194 were DOT 105 cars.

Ownership and lettering

Most major oil companies have owned or leased pressure cars for LPG service. Significant fleets were owned or leased by Cities Service, Gulf, Phillips, Shell, and Warren (which had the largest private fleet, with about 2,000 cars in LPG service in the early 1950s). The era of large lettering and logos had largely ended by the mid-1960s, so most cars from the 1970s onward bear only reporting marks, number, and required data.

Chapter 5 also includes details on the inspection-date matrix, hazardous-material placards, and other required lettering. Placards and commodity stenciling is required on LPG cars — "LIQUEFIED PETROLEUM GAS" with additional "NON ODORIZED" lettering if applicable.

MODELING TIPS

Several manufacturers have offered plastic cars and kits for LPG cars, including early ACF 11,000-gallon LPG cars, plus whalebelly cars in HO and N from Atlas. A modern 33,900-gallon car in HO and N has been made by Athearn Genesis and a modern HO car by Walthers. Also check Shapeways.com and other 3-D printing markets for models of various tank cars.

Be sure you use the appropriate cars when modeling operations and industries. Small pressure cars are used for higher-density chemicals and products and wouldn't be appropriate at an LPG dealer. And make sure you don't park general-service (non-pressure) cars at LPG dealers!

This overall appearance of this DOT 112J340W car built by Union resembles the offset-ladder ARI car to the left, but the design of the saddles, bonnet, upper railing and platform, and end railing and stirrup steps all differ. *Jeff Wilson*

CHAPTER SEVEN

Train operations

A BNSF crude oil unit train passes through the Columbia River Gorge in 2017. Crude shipments by rail rose dramatically in the 2010s with new oilfield discoveries (notably North Dakota's Bakken fields) and technology such as fracking. The covered hopper is an idler car to separate the locomotives from the oil loads.
Scott A. Hartley

American railroads have been involved in moving crude oil and finished petroleum products from the first oil wells and refineries of the 1860s through today. The patterns of train operations have changed through the years, and although pipelines have taken over most of the traffic, railroads continue to serve refineries and their customers.

Early 20th century

Through the 1930s, railroads transported the majority of finished-product traffic from refineries. Railroads delivered empty cars to refineries; picked up loads of gasoline, oil, LPG, and other products; and delivered those loaded cars to local fuel dealers (called "jobbers") across the country, as described in Chapter 3. Most of this was "loose-car" traffic, with individual cars waybilled to various customers.

By the early 1900s, pipelines serving oilfields were carrying most crude oil from wells to refineries. Although railroads continued handling some crude oil traffic, whether a refinery received some or all of its crude by rail varied from refinery to refinery.

As earlier chapters pointed out, tank cars are owned and leased by oil companies, not railroads. This means that a refinery, tank farm, or fuel dealer would receive and ship tank cars owned or leased by a single company (a Sinclair tank car, for example, wouldn't show up at a Shell bulk dealer). An exception was World War II traffic, as we'll see in a bit; oil companies also sold crude and raw refined products amongst themselves, which can result in some intermixing of cars.

A Kansas City Southern RS1 switches the Louisiana & Arkansas yard at New Orleans in the 1940s. Several tank cars are in the yard, including two distinctive UTLX class X cars to the right of the locomotive. *Leon Trice*

World War II

Demand for gasoline and other petroleum products was rising by the end of the 1930s as the Depression began easing. This demand accelerated rapidly with the start of World War II, first as the U.S. began providing supplies to Britain under Lend-Lease, and then when the U.S. officially entered the war after Pearl Harbor in December 1941.

Not only was there suddenly a tremendous demand for fuel (notably high-octane aviation fuel) to be shipped out from ports on both coasts, but the most efficient means of transport—ships from the Gulf coast to ports on the East Coast—was under attack, with German submarines sinking transports within sight of the American coast. These ships, which carried both crude oil to Northeastern refineries as well as finished products, were also now in demand for carrying oil to Europe.

The only other practical solution was shipping by rail. The vast majority of tank cars in the country were placed in service carrying petroleum, mainly from oil fields and refineries in Texas and Oklahoma.

Thousands of older tank cars that had been sitting idle in yards awaiting scrapping were repaired, refurbished, and returned to service. A key to making this move possible was altering how cars were used. As Chapter 5 explained, revenue-service tank cars are privately owned, either by individual oil companies or by leasing companies (who lease them to oil companies and other shippers, who then control

A Sinclair tank car rolls by as a clerk records car numbers at Baltimore & Ohio's Barr Yard in Chicago in 1952. Sinclair had one of the largest fleets of oil-company-owned cars of the steam era. *Wallace W. Abbey*

Railroads carried solid trains of oil and gasoline from the Southwest to Eastern refineries and ports during World War II. This oil train on the Baltimore & Ohio is rolling behind class Q4 2-8-2 No. 4614 in November 1942. *Howard R. Hollem, Library of Congress*

During World War II, a solid train of tank cars, including general-purpose and pressure cars, rolls across the Erie's bridge over the Delaware River at Mill Rift, Pa. *Erie Railroad*

their movements). With dozens of large refining companies involved, this would have made a large-scale, coordinated operation impossible or highly cumbersome, as, for example, Sinclair tank cars would have to be switched only to Sinclair refineries, Phillips cars only to Phillips refineries, and so on.

The solution was to place all tank cars in a pool, allowing them to be routed to any refinery or terminal as needed without regard to ownership. This was enabled by the formation of the Petroleum Administration for War, formed by President Roosevelt in May 1941 and headed by Secretary of the Interior Harold Ickes. The key in implementing the service was that it was coordinated not by a governmental body, but by 450 industry executives representing all of the oil companies involved, with backgrounds in all areas of the industry. Government representatives met with various committees that were formed, utilizing even more individuals with specialized skills and knowledge of the involved industries and railroads. They worked out solutions for coordinating production and transportation of the many needed products among oil companies and individual refineries.

Tank cars in low-mileage regional service, including thousands of cars delivering fuel from refineries and regional tank terminals to dealers averaging under 250 miles per trip, were pulled from that service and moved to the long-haul pool. Truck transports, which pre-war would typically would handle routes of under 100 miles, were assigned to deliver products to 200 or even 300 miles, replacing the tank cars. Only tank cars deemed essential (generally serving routes of 300 miles or more) were allowed to remain in domestic distribution service.

Railroads were soon operating solid trains of tank cars, mainly toward the Northeast but to Pacific ports, as well. By 1943, railroads were carrying a million barrels of oil per day to Eastern ports alone. Demands in the Pacific were lower: 20,000 bbls/day in mid-1943, growing to 170,000 bbls/day by early 1945. Railroads agreed to haul the resulting trains as priority freights—no small task, since other wartime traffic had most railroad routes operating at capacity.

Trains were long and heavy, ranging from 50 to 100 cars, and dispatching was a challenge. Petroleum trains

Oil and gasoline cars would travel in solid cuts in regular manifest freight trains if traffic didn't warrant a dedicated train during the war. Wartime petroleum traffic is beginning to ramp up as this group of cars rolls near Wichita, Kan., in September 1941. *Marion Post Wolcott, Library of Congress*

There was lots of rail action and switching at Standard Oil's Baltimore refinery during World War II, including switching the crude oil and butane unloading racks (foreground). *Standard Oil Co.*

were usually operated as extras or as additional sections of existing trains. Railroads had to coordinate handing off these trains to each other with as little switching or terminal time as possible.

A total of 74,000 tank cars were in this service at the peak of operations. Gas rationing helped curtail domestic demand (and saved valuable rubber resources), and coordinated efforts of refineries and railroads increased production 30 percent over the duration of the war.

Completion of two major pipelines from the Southwest to Northeast in 1943 and 1944 (see Chapter 4) eased demands, but railroads continued operating solid tank car trains until the end of hostilities.

Postwar traffic

Following the war, tank cars were released back to their owners and lessors. However, as the expanded pipeline network also reverted to domestic service, the need for railroad transport of finished products began dropping dramatically from the late 1940s onward.

The oldest cars that had served through the war were retired and scrapped (mostly older ARA I and II cars), followed by other older cars with major mechanical problems. Few new petroleum cars would be built until the size and weight capacity increases of the late 1950s and early 1960s.

Most rail traffic to bulk fuel dealers and jobbers had ended by the late 1960s and early 1970s, and many tank terminals had become truck-served only by that time, as well. Refineries were still served by rail, with most outbound products heading to industrial customers. Some LPG dealers remained served by rail. Most of this traffic was single-car shipments or cuts of multiple cars.

Crude oil operations into the early 2000s were limited (under 10,000 carloads per year), but active in specific regions and routes. As an example, Southern Pacific from 1983 to 1997 ran trains of crude from the San Joaquin Valley near Bakersfield southward through the Tehachapis to a Shell refinery near Los Angeles. (A pipeline replaced trains on this route in 1997.) The trains were nicknamed "Oil Cans."

Modern crude traffic

The development of fracking and other drilling methods that enabled expansion of oil fields that had been limited or unrecoverable opened up the opportunity for railroads to begin hauling large amounts of crude oil starting in the 2010s. New fields in North Dakota (Bakken shale) and in Alberta (tar sands) north of the border began producing large amounts of oil, and with no ready pipeline access to the fields, it was up to railroads to carry it to refineries in various parts of the U.S.

Operational regulations

The longstanding basic rule in the U.S. is that a car carrying hazardous materials of most classes (most petroleum products) is to be placed no fewer than six cars behind a locomotive or ahead of a caboose. If there are not sufficient non-hazardous cars in the train to do this, then all buffer cars must be placed between the placarded cars and locomotive (or, if there's an occupied caboose, available buffer cars must be equally divided between the placarded cars and the locomotive and caboose).

However, in the case of unit trains, the Federal Railroad Administration allows using a single buffer car, usually an older covered hopper filled with ballast or sand to provide a weight similar to the trailing loads. The National Transportation Safety Board in 2020 recommended that at least five buffer cars be required, a proposal also endorsed by the Brotherhood of Locomotive Engineers and Trainmen. However, no action had been taken as of early 2023.

Hazardous materials fall under several categories, but all cars carrying them (including petroleum products) must be placarded. Since the 1970s, placards include the UN number and the specific class of product. For example, gasoline is No. 1203, a red placard, and is a Class 3 flammable liquid.

Other train operation rules specify how cars of various classes are handled, including train speed, which is 50 mph for "Key Trains," which are defined by containing hazardous materials cars in various numbers and combinations. The complete rules are specified in detail in the AAR publication *U.S. Hazardous Materials Instructions for Rail.*

Two Baltimore & Ohio EMD Geeps pull 10 loads of crude oil from a small oil well loadout on a branch line east of Mineral City, Ohio, in 1977. The B&O operation was typical of small-scale well operations that didn't justify a pipeline. Operations ran from 1970 to 1984. *John E. Beach*

A Reading & Northern local switches cars at Koppy's Propane in Good Spring, Pa., in 2017 (also see page 53). Many local fuel dealers switched to all-truck deliveries by the late 1960s, but some larger dealers (especially LPG jobbers) still receive loads by rail. *Scott A. Hartley*

The introduction of General American's TankTrain system in 1977 helped lead to unit-train operation. This fuel oil train on Grand Trunk Western in 1978 is 60 cars long (each 23,100 gallons), with cars divided into four 15-car groups. It travels between a Canadian refinery and a Michigan power plant. *George Drury*

Crude shipments by rail in the U.S. jumped from 11,000 carloads in 2009 to 60,000 in 2011, 234,000 in 2012, and topped 400,000 in 2013. Even though carloadings have dropped since then, fluctuating with all the variables in the oil market (such as foreign oil availability, crude pricing, and demand by refineries for specific types of crude oil), railroads continue to haul a significant amount of crude oil.

Railroads haul most of this traffic in unit trains, originating at a specific oil fields and traveling to refineries across the country. Racks allow loading multiple cars, with either loops allowing full trains to be loaded at once, or on long parallel tracks to make it easier to assemble full trains.

Unit train sizes vary, but 80 to 120 cars is typical. This means a 100-car train of 30,000-gallon cars has a capacity of 3 million gallons (71,428 barrels) of oil.

Matching owners to routes

A consideration in modeling historic petroleum traffic is keeping in mind where specific cars traveled. Because revenue-service tank cars were privately owned, they stayed on routes and in regions as their owners or lessees needed them. They weren't like railroad-owned boxcars, which could show up anywhere.

This was especially true into the early diesel era, when there were several oil companies with national reach (Shell, Gulf, Texaco) but dozens of companies that were regional, covering several states.

This isn't a major concern when dealing with tank cars that lack a company logo or name and bear only the reporting marks of a lessor, such as UTLX, Shipper's Car Line, or GATX. The biggest concern is with cars painted with their owners' names or logos, which was most common from the steam era through the 1950s, as Chapters 5 and 6 explain. The Champlin case in Chapter 4 is one example, where a Champlin car in the 1950s would be at home running from Oklahoma through Nebraska and Iowa, but realistically out of place in Florida or Washington.

Oil brands and the regions they appeared in changed often through the years as oil companies merged and spun off other brands, with some regional companies disappearing and others growing to cover more territory. Knowing what oil companies covered the region you model during the period you model will improve your layout's realism both visually and operationally.

You can find much of this information with online research. Period oil company road maps (a common giveaway item into the 1970s) are also a great way to learn details, as they often tout their brand's region or highlight the locations of stations and dealers in the state being shown. These maps are also a great source of logos for layout signs.

Crude oil is transloaded from trucks to tank cars at the Plains Oil Co. loading facility near New Town, N.D., in 2011. The semis gather the oil from storage tanks at well sites. *Charles W. Bohi*

A BNSF unit oil train with mid-train distributed power carries crude from North Dakota oil fields in 2014. *Scott A. Hartley*

CHAPTER EIGHT

Fuel trucks

Railroads sometimes contract with local jobbers to supply diesel fuel for their locomotives. A delivery truck from Ag-One Co-op in Andersonville, Ind., makes a delivery to a CSX GP40-2 with a side-mounted hose reel in the 1990s. *Mont Switzer collection*

Tank trucks have been used to carry fuel and oil among refineries, distributors, dealers, and customers since the early 1900s. They are fascinating, often colorful vehicles, and since they're often seen at fuel dealers and other rail locations, they are great subjects for modeling. They can do a lot to place a scene in a specific time and region, and even a specific city.

As with railcars, fuel trucks have evolved significantly since the early 1900s. Prior to trucks, finished products (kerosene and gasoline) were carried by wagons pulled by teams of two to four horses. These tank wagons appeared with the first oil fields of the 1860s, carrying crude to refineries, and evolved to carry finished products (usually kerosene, then gasoline) from dealers to homes, businesses, and even to early gas stations.

Typical size was from 300 to 800 gallons, with three compartments. Loading was via top hatches, unloading through valves in the rear at the bottom. The driver's seat was usually built into the tank itself. They would often be painted with their owner's name, and sometimes the name of the branded oil company. Wagons remained in service in some areas into the 1920s.

Straight trucks

As soon as motorized trucks became practical, bulk tank bodies began

Horse-drawn tank wagons were the standard method of delivering kerosene and other products into the 1900s, and some dealers continued as late as the 1920s. Later trucks are still often referred to as "tank wagons." *Standard Oil Co.*

appearing. Almost any brand and style of truck could be used, with many early open-cab gasoline and electric trucks in fuel service, followed by closed-cab trucks of all makes.

These early fuel bodies were relatively small, around 600 to 900 gallons, into the 1930s. Most trucks of the era had capacities between 2 and 4 tons; 900 gallons of gasoline weighs 5,400 pounds, or about 2¾ tons, and the tank itself weighed about ¾ ton. The tanks had an elliptical cross section (wider than they are tall), which helped to lower the trucks' center of gravity. Tanks had multiple internal compartments (three to five) of varying sizes, allowing the truck to carry multiple products (two grades of gas, diesel fuel, heating oil, etc.).

Most tank bodies on these early trucks were unshrouded, often with walkways or platforms next to the tank. These platforms could be used to carry packaged products (such as cans or boxes of oil or grease) or containers, and could have side panels that pivoted up and down. Hose connections for unloading were at the rear, with open pipe connections and valves for delivery hose connections.

Meters were yet to be used on trucks, so to measure small amounts (less than a full compartment load), fuel was first poured into regulated 5- and 10-gallon measuring cans (see page 104). These cans were stowed on the side platforms or in a compartment at the rear of the tank.

This circa-1925 Texaco truck on a Mack chassis has a three-compartment tank. The side platforms have swing-down doors and can hold products, here containers of Texaco's Thuban lube compound and wood cases of motor cup grease. *Library of Congress*

A truck delivers fuel to a Mobilgas (Socony-Vacuum) station in 1939. Early trucks had exposed connectors at the rear for each tank compartment. The cans in the rear compartment were for measuring fuel before trucks were equipped with meters. *Russell Lee, Library of Congress*

A dramatic change in body styles emerged in the mid-1930s as Dodge introduced what it called the "Airflow" design, a streamlined, Art Deco style used by Texaco and others. Soon International, Diamond T, and other builders were offering similar designs.

Although full streamlining didn't remain popular, tanks did retain lower shrouding extending downward from the walkways, which allowed access to the tank roof (see the Champlin truck on page 65 in Chapter 4). At the top were hatches above each compartment (usually three to five), allowing access for loading. The entire top was surrounded by a rub rail to contain any spills that occurred while loading, and also to provide protection to the hatches and tank top in case of a rollover accident.

A rear compartment enclosed the valves, hose connections, and pump, and a meter was now standard, eliminating the need for measuring cans. This compartment was accessed through a door at the rear, usually a wide one that hinged upward. Some truck bodies had a pair of doors hinged on their sides, but the upward-hinging door was better for protecting equipment and the driver in bad weather. An additional delivery hose reel was usually located in a side compartment ("belly box") behind the shrouding, as were additional storage areas that could be used for tools or packaged products.

Tank size continued growing, with 1,000-gallon capacity by the 1940s,

Until trucks were equipped with meters, they carried cans to measure various quantities of fuel for delivery. They can often be spotted along the sideboards of older trucks. This is a five-gallon measuring can of Standard Oil of Indiana. *Two photos: Mont Switzer*

A small tank semi with a five-compartment, single-axle trailer is parked in New Orleans in 1943. A variety of measuring cans rests on the sideboard. *Library of Congress*

A tandem-axle, eight-compartment trailer makes a delivery to a Standard station in Tracy, Calif., in 1942. The modern trailer (for the period) features streamlined styling. *John Vachon, Library of Congress*

Streamlining was coming to fuel truck bodies by the late 1930s. This Standard tank, on a tandem-axle GMC chassis, has side sheathing and distinctive stand-alone side lettering. The dealer is leading a scrap rubber drive near Detroit in 1942, with temporary lettering on the cab and tank sides. *Arthur S. Siegel, Library of Congress*

This Ruan trailer typifies large delivery trailers from the late 1950s through the 1960s, with broad, rounded nose (to allow clearance to a close-coupled cab), side-mounted hose and control connections, and simple, curved mud guard over the wheels. This truck is making a delivery to a Standard station in Iowa in 1957. *Ken Scarpino; Mont Switzer collection*

1,600-gallon tanks by the 1960s, and 2,100-gallon tanks by the 1980s. The body style also continued evolving, with the shrouding continuing farther upward and the tank body itself getting taller (when looking at photos, compare the tank height to the cab roof). The individual compartment capacities are usually stenciled on the rub rails at top of the sides.

By the 1990s, many bodies with tandem axles were approaching 3,000 gallons, and the body style had evolved to again eliminate shrouding.

Most straight trucks (which are still often known as "tank wagons") are in delivery service, owned by fuel dealers and local jobbers, or by local drivers who are contracted to haul for the jobber. Most are not ornately adorned and were typically simple, with painted wheels and grills instead of chrome, and lacking the fancy details found on many owner-operator big rigs.

They are typically painted in the scheme of the oil company they serve, with logos, and may carry additional lettering indicating the local fuel dealer name (with city and phone number, of course). Don't forget warning signs and labels ("This vehicle stops at all railroad crossings," "Inflammable").

As trucks (conventional and tractor-trailers) evolved, their features varied based on whether their purpose was delivery (multiple stops at gas stations, homes, and other customers) or transport (getting as much fuel as possible from one point to another).

Tractor-trailers

Tank tractor-trailers since the 1930s have been most commonly used for longer hauls from refineries and tank terminals, but have also been used by some high-volume local dealers for local delivery service.

Early semis could be found with single- and twin-axle trailers, but by the late 1950s two-axle trailers became the standard to maximize the payload. Sizes ranged from 3,000 on early trailers to 6,000 gallons by the 1960s; modern trailers are typically around 9,500 gallons, but can be larger depending on state weight regulations. As with straight trucks, tank trailers have multiple compartments, with three, four, or five being common.

Tank trailers carrying fuel typically have elliptical cross sections. The top has skid rails surrounding the domes, designed both to contain any spills as well as to protect the domes, hatch covers, and top of the tank in a rollover accident.

Through the 1960s, most fuel tank trailers were steel. The front end was rounded broadly, providing turning clearance when the kingpin was positioned deep, allowing the front of the tank to be very close to the rear of the cab (see the Ruan truck on the previous page). This minimized the overall tractor-trailer length for clearance. The front often had protruding or recessed steps for roof access.

Early trailers had shrouding around the rear wheels and rear of the tank, much like straight trucks. The delivery hose, control valves, and meter were behind a door on the rear, or in a

Shelby Petroleum in Greenfield, Ind., operated this delivery truck with a Ford C cabover chassis in the 1980s. The modern-style tank lacks the side platforms of earlier tanks, since modern loading racks allow direct roof access. *Mont Switzer collection*

The back compartment houses meters, pumps, and control equipment. The flip-up rear door provides protection to the equipment and operator in bad weather. *Mont Switzer collection*

Weight regulations regarding length in some states resulted in semi tractors with extended frames, such as this 1950s-era truck. Modeling features like this can greatly increase realism by matching prototype practice in specific states, regions, and eras. *Jeff Wilson collection*

To maximize payload while complying with length/weight restrictions, a common setup for transport trucks in California was a large tandem-axle straight truck pulling a trailer. This Shell tank rides on a Peterbilt chassis in the 1970s. *Jeff Wilson collection*

This modern Switzer Tank Lines semi is set up as a portable station to provide fuel for races. It's at Elkhart Lake, Wis., in 2023. Note the side reflective striping, side-mounted delivery connections, top rub rails, and flatter nose compared to earlier trailers. *Mont Switzer collection*

closed belly box below the tank on one side. Designs became more open by the 1960s.

By the 1970s, the trend was toward aluminum tanks, which were lighter and, with revised weight and clearance laws, larger. Trailer fronts were no longer broadly rounded, but slightly convex, with conventional kingpin placement. Gone was the access door at the rear, replaced by the tank end and bumper. Hose connections, valves, and metering are under the tank at the side, usually in the open. Long tubes along the lower sides of the tank hold the delivery hose. A roof access ladder typically runs up the middle of the back.

Older trucks with steel tanks were painted in company colors. Aluminum tanks are often left natural and polished, with the brand name and/or local dealer or jobber name displayed prominently, usually using decals.

Tractors in fuel service were typically designed for short hauls compared to over-the-road van operations, so they usually lack sleeper units. They also often lack the ornamentation of many long-haul tractors. Conventional and cabover tractors were both used, but as with other trucks, the move was to conventional tractors by the 1990s.

In California and some other states, regulations on truck length and bridge weight loading created some interesting vehicle variations. Many tractors had extra-long frames, with a large gap between the rear of the cab and the nose of the trailer. Another common Western variation to avoid that gap and make more efficient use of length was a three-axle straight truck with tank pulling a two- or three-axle tank trailer (single axle in front, one or two axles in rear), with the trailer short enough to match length restrictions. These trailers used a pintle hook connection to the truck instead of a typical semi's fifth-wheel connection.

Check prototype photos for the era and region you model to see what is appropriate for what you're modeling.

LPG trucks

As chapters 3 and 6 discussed, liquified petroleum gas (LPG), a mixture of propane and butane, began being marketed as a home heating fuel in the early 1930s. As local LPG dealers began appearing, especially in small towns and rural areas where natural gas pipelines didn't reach, dealers needed trucks to deliver the product to customers.

Most early home installations used pairs of vertical 100-gallon "bottle" tanks, and LPG dealers swapped out the new tanks during deliveries. These require a stake-bed or van truck to carry the tanks. By the 1940s and '50s, it was becoming more common for homes to have permanent 500-gallon tanks. These required bulk trucks to refill them.

The pressure tanks on these bulk trucks are cylindrical with hemispherical ends, placed lengthwise on the truck chassis. Early trucks sometimes had pairs of smaller tanks placed side by side, creating a lower center of gravity than a single large tank. By the 1960s, single large tanks were typical, with

MODELING TIPS

Several manufacturers, notably Mini-Metals, have marketed fuel delivery trucks with a variety of prototype oil company paint schemes. You can personalize these by using decal or dry-transfer lettering to add the name of the local fuel dealer or jobber on the cab or body. Walthers offered an older LPG body in a resin kit, and Showcase Miniatures has sold a modern LP truck.

Not as many semi trailers have been offered. Mini-Metals has offered some, and there are older models from Wiking and Ulrich, but they require some work. Trucks 'n' Stuff has offered modern gasoline and LPG trailers, as has Herpa. Also check 3-D printed models through Shapeways.com and other services.

The large transport trucks serving tank terminals in over-highway service tend to be newer models, but many local jobbers (especially through the 1960s and 1970s) used their equipment for a long time, as local delivery trucks didn't pile up mileage like highway trucks. This provides a good opportunity to model older vehicles realistically. As an example, if you model 1970, perhaps a local jobber has a larger brand-new 1970 delivery truck, an older, smaller 1963 model, and an even-older 1956 truck as a backup. Larger businesses will have more trucks.

Remember to add hazmat placards (as described in the chapters on tank cars). A truck being loaded or unloaded at a terminal or gas station, with wire hoses in place and the driver overseeing operations, would make for an interesting scene (see page 51).

Early LPG trucks often had pairs of tanks side-by-side on the truck chassis. Dealers often sold and serviced appliances and furnaces, as well. *Mont Switzer collection*

This new 1960 Dodge truck has a single-tank LPG body. The delivery hose reel is mounted on the rear platform. *Jeff Wilson collection*

This modern LPG trailer has side-mounted hose connections and storage tubes for hoses along the body. *Mont Switzer*

larger capacity than earlier trucks. For either, a hose reel at the rear of the chassis was used to deliver the fuel.

Tractor-trailers are mainly used to deliver fuel to dealers (and sometimes to larger industrial users). These feature similar, but longer, tanks with larger capacity, generally with tandem rear axles.

Other vehicles

Don't forget additional vehicles found at jobbers, tank terminals, and refineries. Examples include stake-bed bodies for delivering 55-gallon drums and LPG tanks, panel trucks, step vans, and enclosed van bodies for maintenance and service calls. Many local jobbers also installed and serviced fuel-oil furnaces and LP furnaces and appliances. And a pickup truck or two in company colors are appropriate for general work or sales calls.

Selected bibliography

Books

Car Builders' Cyclopedia, various editions
Commodities by Freight Car, by Jeff Wilson. Kalmbach Media, 2023.
Freight Cars of the '40s and '50s, by Jeff Wilson. Kalmbach Publishing Co., 2015.
Freight Traffic Red Book, various editions
GATX Tank Car Manual, Third Edition, General American Transportation Corp., 1972.
A Great Name in Oil: Sinclair Through 50 Years, Sinclair Oil Company, 1966.
Modern Freight Cars, by Jeff Wilson. Kalmbach Publishing Co., 2019.
The Official Railway Equipment Register, various editions
Steam Era Freight Cars Reference Manual, Volume 2, Tank Cars, Speedwitch Media, 2008.
Tank Car Color Guide, Volumes 1 and 2, by James Kinkaid. Morning Sun, 2010, 2011.
Tank Cars: American Car & Foundry Co., 1865 to 1955, by Edward Kaminski. Signature Press, 2003.
UTLX Steam Era Tank Cars, by Stephen Hile, Speedwitch Media, 2018.

Periodicals

"AC&F 8,000-Gallon Riveted Tank Cars," by Richard Hendrickson, *RailModel Journal*, October 1997, p. 26.
"AC&F Type 21 Tank Cars, Part II: 10,000-Gallon Cars," by Richard Hendrickson, *RailModel Journal*, January 2000, p. 13.
"AC&F Type 27, 8,000-Gallon, Three-Dome Tank Cars," by Richard Hendrickson, *RailModel Journal*, June 2008, p. 15.
"AC&F Type 27, 10,500-Gallon, ICC-105A Propane Tank Cars," by Ed Hawkins, *Railway Prototype Cyclopedia, Vol. 7*, p. 85.
"All Oiled Up," by Fred W. Frailey, *Trains*, March 2014, p. 26.
"America's First Successful Tank Car," by Richard Senges, *Mainline Modeler*; Part 1, May 2004, p. 56; Part 2, June 2004, p. 32.
"America's Energy Independence Rides the Rails," by Roy Blanchard, *Trains*, June 2009, p. 44.
"Build an 1880s Oil Refinery," by Don Ball, *Model Railroader*, August 2012, p. 28.
"The Champlins and Oklahoma Crude," by David Burr, *Sooner Magazine*, March 1952, p. 8.
"Crude by Rail Under Scrutiny," *Trains*, June 2015, p. 6.
"Crude Oil 101," by Steve Sweeney, *Trains*, October 2013, p. 19.
"Five New Facts to Know About Crude by Rail," by Fred W. Frailey, *Trains*, April 2015, p. 38.
"Fifties-Era Welded Tank Cars," by Richard Hendrickson, *RailModel Journal*, April 1996, p. 52.
"ICC 105 11,000-Gallon High-Pressure Tank Cars," by Richard Hendrickson, *RailModel Journal*, July 2003, p. 48.
"Model an LP Gas Plant on a Curve," by Cody Grivno, *Model Railroader*, August 2011, p. 26.
"Modeler's Guide to Hazardous Material Markings, A," by Matt Snell, *Model Railroader*, May 2010, p. 42.
"Modeler's Guide to Transition-Era Tank Cars," by Tony Koester, *Model Railroader*, December 2008, p. 42.
"Modeling '50s-Era Tank Cars," by Richard Hendrickson, *RailModel Journal*, August 1996, p. 14.
"Modeling 1950s Tank Trailers," by Mont Switzer, *Mainline Modeler*, December 1994, p. 56.
"Modern Tank Cars," by John J. Ryczkowski, *Mainline Modeler*; Part 1: February 1992, p. 58; Part 2: May 1992, p. 71.
"NTSB Raises Buffer Car Concerns," by R.G. Edmonson, *Trains*, May 2017, p. 10.
"Oil Boom (Refined)," by Bill Stephens, *Trains*, March 2018, p. 7.
"Oil Dealer Depots," *RailModel Journal*, March 1997, p. 10.
"Peru Propane Corp.," by Peter A. Cook, *Model Railroader*, March 1980, p. 74.
"Petroleum Terminals," by Mike Small, *Model Railroader*, August 2002, p. 64.
"Pressure Tank Cars, Part IV," by John Ryczkowski, *Mainline Modeler*, November 1992, p. 46.
"Shipping Butane by Rail," by Clifton Linton, *Railroad Model Craftsman*, December 2019, p. 46.
"Tank Car Qualification Stencils," by Stuart Streit, *Railroad Model Craftsman*, September 2002, p. 83.
"Tank Cars," by David Casdorph, *Model Railroading*, February 1995, p. 50.
"Tank Cars: Modeling Non-Pressure Cars," by John Ryczkowski, *Mainline Modeler*, June 1992, p. 48.
"TankTrain Tete-a-Tete," by George Drury, *Trains*, October 1978, p. 16.
"Whalebelly Car," by James Kinkaid, *Mainline Modeler*, May 1997, p. 41.

Miscellaneous

American Association of Railroads (AAR) Rail Time Indicators Report, Feb. 7, 2020.
AAR, Crude Oil Loads on Class I Railroads, 2005-2013.
AAR, Field Guide to Tank Cars, Fourth Edition, 2022.
AAR, Freight Commodity Statistics, Class I Rail Traffic, 1980 vs. 2000 vs. 2020
AAR, USDOT 2015 Rule for Tougher Tank Car Standards
AAR, United States Hazardous Materials Instructions for Rail, 2022
American Oil & Gas Historical Society, aoghs.org
The Anatomy of a Tank Car, General American
U.S. Department of Transportation (DOT), Bureau of Transportation Statistics, various reports
U.S. DOT, Fleet Composition of Rail Tank Cars Carrying Flammable Liquids, multiple annual reports